# Serpent Imagery and Symbolism

# SERPENT IMAGERY

## AND

# SYMBOLISM

*A Study of the Major English Romantic Poets*

Lura Nancy Pedrini

Duilio T. Pedrini

COLLEGE & UNIVERSITY PRESS · *Publishers*

NEW HAVEN, CONN.

*Copyright © 1966 by College and University Press Services, Inc.*

All Rights Reserved

Library of Congress Catalog Card Number: 66-14826

MANUFACTURED IN THE UNITED STATES OF AMERICA BY
UNITED PRINTING SERVICES, INC.
NEW HAVEN, CONN.

# Foreword

THE SERPENT stood for sex eons before the tiger stood for Princeton. To the student of psychological dynamics, it scarcely occurs that snake-symbol can be other than sex-symbol. So some sort of obeisance should be shown to Drs. Lura and Duilio Pedrini for demonstrating that there is more to snake-symbolism than sexuality. They see, and so state specifically, the substratum of sex symbols (principally unconscious); but they find, in their higher strata, conscious symbols in which the snake stands for such diverse ideas as evil, benevolence, reason, sensuousness—the attributes of both idealism and materialism.

The snake as a symbol, for man's purposes, is a world-encompassing subject, one as difficult to grasp figuratively, as to grasp a living snake in reality; perhaps any discussion should be hissed snake-fashion—low-toned, in the alliterative long lines of Anglo-Saxon verse. But from the sacred asp to Jormungand, the Midgard Serpent, the theme of sexuality underlies the snake-lore of the Occident.

The serpent of Eden has always been recognizable as a symbol of sex. The first thing the man and woman did after they obtained the knowledge of good and evil was to recognize themselves as naked and make themselves aprons (to hide their genitalia). And it has been freely assumed, if it has not been an article of faith, that the sex act was the original sin in Eden for which the unredeemed children of Adam are still being punished. Yet if the snake is sex, sex is the reproduction of life, and the snake is thus a symbol of life—of continuing life, of everlasting life. It has so been recognized, for good or evil, from time immemorial.

The sex symbolism of the snake seems to rest primarily on the fact that the serpent, with head erect, ready to strike, resembles the erect phallus. Certain snakes also expand head or neck, when in a striking position, to add to the likeness. The snake as a sex symbol is, of course, a deity. He is a deity because the phallus is also a deity, the magical giver of life. And the snake is a deity because, besides being a phallus, he sheds his skin instead of dying, crawls out resplendent in a new one, and so lives forever. He is a deity because when he is pictured with his tail in his mouth, he forms a circle, a line never broken and so a sign of eternity; as such, he may be symbolized in a finger-ring, a magic circle for divining, or the serpent who girds Midgard. He is also a chthonic symbol of great power; he originates in the earth, coming from a hole in it and returning to a hole in it (also sexual symbolism); he has access to the secrets of birth and death, and so of the underworld. As a knower of the unknown, the snake is also a figure of wisdom, like the snake of Eden, and a figure of healing, as possessed of the knowledge to drive out disease.

Aaron's rod turned into a serpent to impress Pharaoh with the power of the LORD. Then the wise men, sorcerers and physicians of Egypt cast down their rods, which also became serpents; but Aaron's serpent ate the Egyptian serpents.[1] When the LORD sent fiery serpents to punish the children of Israel because they grumbled in the wilderness, the serpents bit the people, and "much people of Israel died." Then Moses, at the LORD's direction, made a fiery serpent of his own out of brass and "put it upon a pole, and it came to pass, that if a serpent had bitten any man, when he beheld the serpent of brass, he lived."[2] Israel might not worship God in the guise of a bull or "golden calf," but veneration of the serpent was another matter. Some authorities believe that the ark of the covenant, far from being empty, contained a brazen serpent.[3] At any rate, Hezekiah, the reform king of Judah, who "did *that which was* right in the sight of the LORD," "brake in pieces the brasen serpent that Moses had made: for unto those days the children of Israel did burn incense to it . . ."[4]

[1] Exodus 7: 8-12.
[2] Numbers 21: 6-9.
[3] A. Powell Davies, *The Ten Commandments* (New York: New American Library, Signet Key Book).
[4] 2 Kings 18: 3, 4.

These Biblical serpents were phallic. Whether or no they possessed attributes of the Deity—and they were certainly at least conceived as His supernatural representatives—they were identical with the serpent-gods openly worshiped by the peoples neighboring to Israel. Further, Aaron's rod was a recognizable phallic symbol before it became a serpent, and the pole on which Moses hoisted the serpent of brass was such as many Near Eastern peoples worshiped (and one need not even go to the Near East but merely consider the Maypole).

Besides special psychiatric interest in symbolism of all sorts, medicine in general has interest in snake symbolism, as the sign of Asclepius, god of healing, whose image, holding a curative serpent, was set among the stars by Zeus.[5] Asclepius' snake and staff were a double sexual (and healing) symbol: but modern medicine has redoubled it—evidently on the theory that if one serpent is good, two are better—by substituting the serpent-entwined caduceus of Hermes, originally decorated with heraldic white ribbons that were later mistaken for snakes because Hermes was herald to Hades.[6] Furthermore, when the ribbons were mistaken for snakes, the snakes were conceived to be copulating—a most potent addition to the caduceus' magical properties—though natural history[7] testifies that snakes copulate in a different, and far less picturesque, fashion. Asclepius' snakes, as distinguished from Hermes', took an active part in bestowing their healing power (ultimately derived from sexual power) by crawling among the suppliants sleeping at his shrines.[8]

Medicine has other interests in the snake cult. Apollo, divine patron of medicine, established his shrine at Delphi where he slew the great serpent, Python.[9] Apollo, perforce, continued his connection with the slain snake-god by becoming patron, by order

[5] Robert Graves, *The Greek Myths* (Baltimore: Penguin Books, 1955), I, 175. (Citing ancient authorities.)

[6] *Ibid.*, p. 66.

[7] James A. Oliver, *Snakes in Fact and Fiction* (New York: Macmillan, 1958), p. 122.

[8] For a modern fictional treatment of this theme, see Gladys Mitchell, *Come Away Death* (Harmondsworth, Middlesex, England: Penguin Books, Ltd., 1954).

[9] Graves, *op. cit.*, I, 76.

of Zeus, of the Pythian games instituted to honor Python's memory. Further, the sacred tripod on which the priestess of the Delphic Oracle sat, was supported by intertwined snakes.[10] (It still exists to bear witness, as it was stolen from Delphi by that notable Christian, Constantine the Great, to decorate his new imperial capital.)

To round out this elementary survey, it should be remarked that the serpent with its sex symbolism has figured in magic and religion all around the world. In Voodoo, a religion with marked sexuality, the serpent is actually worshiped in the western world in modern times.[11] Worship of the snake exists or has existed among widely diverse peoples from India to Yucatan. And it seems not at all unlikely that the snakes which legend says St. Patrick expelled from Ireland were sacred serpents, perhaps accompanied into exile by their priests and worshipers.

It should be noted, too, that the snake, though always sexual, is not always masculine. Medusa's head is a fearful object, whether in Perseus' hand, on Athene's aegis, or engraved on an amulet to avert the evil eye. Medusa's head, it is pretty well established, represents the female genitalia[12]—at once an attraction and a symbol of castration to the male.

It would be interesting if one could get the serpent's side of all this. The only attempt to do so that occurs to mind is T. H. White's in that curious saga of King Arthur, of which *The Sword in the Stone* forms the introduction. "The Wart," in the temporary guise of a grass snake, hears from a real one the tragic history of the reptilian race. The last Atlantosaurus immanis, a gigantic but timid lady vegetarian who "had never killed in her life," had the misfortune to meet a human specimen of the subclass Homo sapiens armatus, order of georgius sanctus; and Homo sapiens armatus georgius sanctus "killed her, of course," since he was so unobservant as to classify all dinosaurs together

[10] *Encyclopaedia Britannica.* 14th edition. Vol. 7, p. 174, article on Delphi.

[11] E. Royston Pike, *Encyclopedia of Religion and Religions* (New York: Meridian, 1958), p. 346.

[12] Sigmund Freud, "Medusa's Head," in *Collected Papers* (New York: Basic Books, 1959), V, 107.

(harmless as well as dangerous) as his enemies.[13] One has the feeling that there should be a moral in this; but inasmuch as the Wart, magicked into a snake by Merlin, did not crawl into a hole to hibernate and dream about it in his slow snake mind but became King of England instead, the story seems somewhat inconclusive. If the Wart's friend had known that Homo sapiens, of whatever subclass and order, regarded the serpent with fear and awe because of its fortuitous resemblance to the erect human phallus, he would probably have considered it another of the mysterious misfortunes which nature had inflicted on the reptilian race.

The testimony could be multiplied to infinity that the serpent has long been recognized as a phallic symbol. It was, of course, one of almost innumerable such symbols. One can go well before Freud to find modern recognition of what was once considered a shameful matter; and one should do so, for Freud's interpretations in this field are regarded with skeptical prejudice by too many persons who should be better informed. Richard Payne Knight wrote a discussion of the worship of Priapus in 1786, a book which met with such a violent reception it had to be withdrawn from publication. (He found a survival of Priapus worship in the cult of Saints "Cosmo and Damiano" in what was then the Kingdom of Naples in southern Italy.) Eighty years later, Thomas Wright, inspired thereto by Knight's book, extended the discussion of sex worship, including the female as well as the male principle, to all of western medieval Europe.[14]

Knight lists the snake among many animal and artificial phallic symbols, the bull, the goat (Knight cites Herodotus as reporting actual intercourse between women and goats in Egypt), the ram, the lizard, artifacts ranging from amulets to temple decorations, gods, fawns and satyrs, and, of course, the sun. Wright

---

[13] T. H. White, *The Sword in the Stone* (New York: Putnam's, 1939), p. 182 ff.

[14] Knight's book, *A Discourse on the Worship of Priapus* (1786), and Wright's *The Worship of the Generative Powers* (1866) were reprinted in a single volume under the title of *Sexual Symbolism* in 1957. This book has an introduction by Ashley Montagu and is published by Julian Press, Inc. of New York.

lists the snake, a variety of plants from arum to mandrake to orchid, such phallic gestures as "the fig" or obscene hand, and various religious symbols. He also notes symbols of female sexuality, from the Shelah-na-Gigs[15] found carved over the doors of certain ancient churches to such fruits as the fig, the apricot, and the pomegranate.

An even longer and more impressive list can be found in a small volume on ancient sex worship by a certain Sha Rocco, who also considerably antedated Freud. This author, apparently using a pseudonym in the climate of the Victorian era, wrote his little book in 1874, and it was republished under the same name in 1904[16] by a company that was putting out much "advanced," including socialistic, literature at that time. The author pays due attention to snakes, and he notes other animal phallic symbols, such as the bull, ram, goat and tortoise. But animals hardly represent a start in the way of sex symbolism. Says Rocco: "Obelisks, pillars of any shape, stumps, trees denuded of boughs, upright stones are some of the means by which the male element was symbolized. Siva is represented as a stone standing alone." The letter "T," the torch, fire, a knobbed stick, the crozier, the pre-Christian cross, are other phallic symbols. Towers, spires, minarets, poles, and pine, poplar and palm trees, sometimes accompanied by "eggs, apples or citrons, plums, grapes and the like," serve as other symbols of the male genitalia. Female symbols include holes in the ground, caves and the sea shell sacred to Aphrodite.

There is no scientific doubt of the truth of these interpretations. Those cited here are—except for Medusa's head—all pre-Freudian; and it should be noted that Rocco in particular relies on still earlier authorities for his data. The fact is—as one contributor to *The Psychiatric Quarterly* noted in an informal comment on his own manuscript—that the world is full of hollow things and things that fit into them, and one wonders at times if the business of insisting on sex symbolism cannot be overdone.

[15] Figures of naked women, the genitals exposed and pointed to with the hands.
[16] Sha Rocco, *Ancient Sex Worship* (New York: Commonwealth Co., 1904).

There is no doubt that it is, or was, there; but how many spectators watching a children's dance around a Maypole see the original sex rite; and how many farmers nailing horsehoes (today's equivalent of the Shelah-na-Gigs) above their doorways for luck have an inkling that they are dealing with a sex symbol? The beribboned Maypole is quaint, pretty and full of the happy innocence of childhood; the horseshoe is a half-regarded, half-derided concession to superstition—like knocking on wood, which, incidentally, also has a phallic interpretation.

Sexual symbolism in these and innumerable other instances belongs to remote etiology, not present diagnosis—if it belongs to the present at all, it belongs to the unconscious. The architect does not see a vulva in a Gothic doorway; but he may dream of the doorway as one, recovering from his own unconscious the image some predecessor architect held consciously centuries ago. So, in a dream, or in free association, one may find in the unconscious the church steeple as a symbol of the phallus, or the spider as an emblem of female sexuality. Today, we do not doubt that the unconscious contains much that a worshiper of Priapus or Aphrodite or Dionysius would have recognized consciously 2,000 years in the past.

But sometimes one may wonder whether those of us who are well aware of the wilderness of the unconscious are not too close to it to see the trees of the neatly landscaped conscious. We deal, after all, with the conscious, every waking moment of our beings, and it may be suggested timidly that sometimes the best way to appreciate the conscious is to accept it as it purports to be, not search for the unconscious mechanisms, motivations, symbolisms behind it. This is not therapy, but good socially acceptable behavior.

Even the snake, branded for uncounted centuries as a phallic symbol, has a wealth of other symbolism, as the Pedrinis' discussion demonstrates. The dynamism for its numerous roles may or may not derive from its power in the unconscious as a sex symbol —the probability is that unconscious recognition of the snake as a symbol of a driving, sexual force does have something to do with it—but its other roles in the conscious are well worth psychological as well as literary attention.

The plumed serpent of Yucatan and Mexico is a creation of the unconscious (and presumably not entirely a sexual symbol) as well worth attention as that of China's imperial dragon. So, too, was the famous dragon-ship of the Vikings probably derived from unconscious symbolism, a matter also meriting study. But the eagle grasping a snake in its talons, which signified to the wandering Aztecs that here they should found their city of Tenochtitlan, was presumably a conscious symbol, a sign of triumph in barbarian war.

So also conscious was the symbolism of the rattlesnake as exemplifying the code of the gunfighter of the Old West: "He is a gentleman; he warns before he strikes." And it is perhaps mere accident that the armies and the fighting ships of the United States today do not carry the rattlesnake flag into battle beside the Stars and Stripes. The rattlesnake here was a consciously devised symbol of rebellion and defiance. It decorated the flag of South Carolina, appeared on the flags of our early ships at sea, and was on the banners carried into battle by many a colonial regiment. Typically, such a flag bore a coiled and menacing serpent with 13 rattles and the ominous motto "Don't Tread on Me."

NEWTON BIGELOW, M.D.
G. MONROE WHITE

*The Psychiatric Quarterly*
Utica, New York

# Preface

THE AUTHORS' INTEREST in the serpent imagery and
symbolism in English Romantic poetry began when there was
occasion to study Keats's serpent imagery. Much has been written
about a few special snakes and their pictorial and symbolic value,
but no complete study of all the serpent images in Romantic
poetry has been made. The task in this book has been to arrange
these images and their symbolism into meaningful classifications.
It was felt that the less celebrated and nondescript snakes might
tell us as much about the major Romantics and Romanticism
as the more famous ones, such as Shelley's good serpent in
*The Revolt of Islam,* Coleridge's water snakes in *The Rime of
the Ancient Mariner,* and Keats's serpent-woman in *Lamia.*

Literature concerning snake-worship is abundant, but the Romantics seemed to be concerned primarily with the serpent's sensuous appeal and its evil nature. It is true that the serpent par-
ticipates in their portrayals of a pantheistic world, especially
that of Shelley, but then only as a kindred being deserving consideration, not adoration.

Because so much of the serpent lore seems to have no direct
bearing on the actual imagery and symbolism, background
material and other secondary source material have been kept at
a minimum. Wherever a bit of snake lore has been helpful, it has
been used; wherever secondary sources have helped to explain
the image and symbol in terms of the writers' own classification,
they have been used. But they have been omitted whenever
their use seemed to be forcing information upon the reader and
the image. Since the main concern was to stay closely to the
actual imagery in the Romantic poems, only a third of the
material collected is presented—in an attempt to avoid an
encyclopedic dissertation.

The authors wish to express their gratitude to Dr. Willis Pratt for generosity with time in consultation and constructiveness in criticism, and to Drs. D. T. Starnes, Oscar Maurer, Joseph Jones and R. H. Williams, all of the faculty of the Graduate School of the University of Texas, for co-operation with many helpful suggestions.

LURA NANCY PEDRINI
DUILIO T. PEDRINI

*Omaha, Nebraska*

# Contents

# Serpent Imagery and Symbolism

# I

## Symbolism and Romanticism

THE NINETEENTH-CENTURY ROMANTICISTS were dissatisfied with the cold analytical reasoning of the preceding century and its deadening effect upon literature, art, and life.[1] Stressing the totality of man, they deprecated the understanding, because of its inadequacy to apprehend spiritual truths. The Romanticists acknowledged the power of reason and intellect to dismantle and dissect, but deplored the powerlessness of these faculties to put the pieces back together and to see a unity among them. In *The Tables Turned,* for example, Wordsworth accuses the meddling intellect of being a murderer:

> Sweet is the lore which Nature brings;
> Our meddling intellect
> Misshapes the beauteous forms of things,—
> We murder to dissect.[2]

Only imagination, the intuitive faculty, is the synthesizer. Labeling the component parts requires critical acumen; synthesizing them into a unified whole requires the help of the intuitive imagination. Wordsworth in *Intimations of Immortality* dwells at length upon the superiority of the child's intuition over the adult's reason, which leads him away from ultimate truth and its divine source, the spiritual force residing in and energizing all life. Man's traveling into adulthood away from his spiritual home is comparable to the sun's progress through the heavens from its birth to its setting. The farther it advances after noon, the dimmer its light becomes. And unless man can penetrate the

19

darkness with his intuitive imagination, he loses his way; for even though his reason points out the signposts, it is only his imagination which turns the signposts into symbols. Reason, the senses, and understanding apprehend signposts which direct man through the perceptual world; the intuitive imagination interprets the signposts, not as designators, but as symbols which direct man through the spiritual world.

The symbol suggests meanings growing out of thought and feeling that reside in the penumbral area between the brightness of the sun and the darkness of the shadow core. Reason, understanding, and the senses apprehend the signs only in the sunlight; intuition and imagination, the seeing-eye dog of blind reason and understanding, penetrate the shadows and experience a whole new world. In terms of another analogy,

> When we deal with a symbol, it is rather as if we drew the cork from the magic bottle of the Arabian Nights. First a kind of thick and confusing smoke pours out; then strange forms take shape out of the smoke, and modify each other, perceptually shifting in the corners of our mind.[3]

Symbol, like smoke, is at first formless, without body, and indeterminate but is "always the remainder, or reminder, of something that once had intrinsic value, as an image, shadow, or reflection has by being, or participating in, the man's soul."[4] Or symbol, suggesting rather than stating, casting shadows rather than delineating in bold, definitive lines, possesses the construction and quality of "dreams, through which unformed feelings and desires unwittingly find expression."[5] Again resembling smoke, "symbol is distinguished by being focal, massive and not arbitrary."[6] Just as the spectator's imagination can transform the mass of smoke into various shapes, so can this same creative faculty forge numerous and widely divergent meanings out of symbol. The signpost, being arbitrary, requires the complete obedience of reason; the symbol, which is not arbitrary, lends itself to the flexibility and liberating power of intuition and imagination, which turns the material world into a copy of the invisible world. This invisible world is the spiritual, ideal world and can be attained only by power of the intuition and imagination to recognize the signs of the material world as false and deceiving and to accept them as symbols pointing beyond themselves to a more real world than the perceivable one. "The symbolist leaves the given to find that which is more real."[7] The perceivable, given world is an expression of thought, and the symbolist is more interested in the thought which has prompted the expression than in the expression itself.

Ananda Coomaraswamy explains the symbol as man's effort to embody in a tangible or otherwise perceptible form the divine and spiritual, which he cannot understand until he has translated it on a lower level. Coomaraswamy observes that symbols do not increase with the development of higher spirituality in men but, on the contrary, they emerge when there is a decline in our divinity and spirituality. Symbols provide a remedy for the indigence of the soul in the time of decline. Cautioning against the formalistic method of investigating the outward and formal aspects of symbols—an approach which leads to a vacuum since it deals with the end, not with the beginning—Coomaraswamy particularly exhorts the creative artist to penetrate beyond the tangible:

> Maintain the transparence of the material, that it may be saturated with the spirit. He can obey the command only if he maintains his own transparency, and that is the rock on which most of us are apt to break. Each and everyone reaches a point in life when he begins to stiffen and—either [sic] stiffens in fact or must by superhuman effort recover for himself what he possessed undiminished in his childhood but was more and more taken from him in youth; so that the doors of the spiritual world may open to him, and the spirit find its way into body and soul.[8]

Literary symbols originated as truly social products. The central function of poetry as symbolism is the poet's attempt to formulate into language, and to elucidate, his experiences so that society can share and better understand those thoughts, feelings, and instincts common to all mankind. In Freudian terms, Ernest Jones observes that symbolism, particularly unconscious symbolism, is "confined to the themes of birth, love and death, and to

thoughts about the body and the nearest relatives."[9] Jones concludes that these themes must comprise the fundamental interests
of mankind. The restrictions of society render a man unable or
unwilling to express freely some of his feelings and ideas, even
though they are common to all people; therefore, symbolism is
the individual's way of overcoming these inhibitions and restrictions to share thoughts and feelings with society which it already
possesses but for which society would punish him, provided he
spoke literally and directly.

Not every man has the urge or recognizes his power to share
his experiences. All men possess the intuitive faculty, but some
fail to recognize this power, which then remains latent. Others
realize that they themselves are miniature divinities, possessing
the capacity for penetrating the great energizing source of the
world and for perceiving the truth about actual living experience:

> ... man can never know the truth about himself, nor find in
> his relationships with the world that truth or reality which
> transcends them, unless he develops his power of intuition.
> The intuitive imagination, which works through symbols, is
> the very essence of art.[10]

The assumption with which the symbolist sets out is that there
is a complete break between the natural and the spiritual worlds.
Ascertaining truth involves bridging the gap between the two
worlds. For bridging them, the mystic uses symbols taken from
the natural world which the senses apprehend but can only par-
tially interpret. The senses cannot go beyond a literal translation of the material world. Man's intuition must finish the process of the action initiated by the senses and envision the whole
picture rather than the partial one. Mystics believe that the soul's
native realm is the spiritual world but that man's whole range
of experiences and observations is limited to the natural world.
Of course, adjustment to the requirements of the natural world
is necessary, but this adaptation must be done without permitting
the spiritual faculties to rust. Even though the mystic recognizes
the division between the natural and spiritual worlds, he still realizes that the former is founded upon the latter and, consequently,
that all of its forms and processes have their counterpart there.

The phenomena of the natural world are valueless unless used to direct attention to the spiritual world. If man accepts the natural world as valuable within and for itself, then he is in a lamentable condition, or, as Blake (following the Bible or Milton) specifically represents him, he is under the spell of a deceiving serpent.

All of the Romanticists felt a symbolism in natural objects, in which they intuited an essence that corresponded to their own essential nature. Out of this correspondence grew a better understanding of themselves and of the whole related world of both the animate and inanimate. Coleridge wrote: "In looking at objects of Nature, ... I seem rather to be seeking, as it were *asking* for, a symbolical language for something within me that already and for ever exists, than observing anything new."[11] This is a typical expression of the Romanticists, who looked for a phenomenon of nature to express their own inner feelings. When Shelley, in his *Ode to the West Wind,* wishes to be a leaf to blow about the earth, a cloud to float through the heavens, or a wave to surge under the power of the Wild Spirit, both creator and destroyer, he is projecting his inner experiences upon actuality. With this tendency to find in natural objects an expression of his inner life, there seems little doubt that Coleridge felt in wind and in stagnant calm symbols of the contrasted states he felt so poignantly, of ecstasy and of inertia.

C. S. Lewis states in *The Allegory of Love* that the poetry of symbolism finds its greatest expression in the time of the Romantics, who recognized this material, visible world as only a copy of the immaterial, invisible world. The concrete, physical objects are imperfect replicas of the abstract, spiritual, and perfect Forms in the other world. In other words, this world is but an imperfect shadow cast by the perfect light of the other world, and the senses, reason, and understanding are inadequate in recognizing the limitations of the shadow world. If one desires to penetrate the essence of being and existence, to apprehend the perfect Forms which cast the shadows, then one must interpret the signs of this world by use of the intuitive imagination rather than by perception. Power to read the symbols lies within the individual's ability to intuit the Oneness in the universe and to participate in this natural order.

What the eighteenth-century rationalists saw as irreconcilable elements, the Romanticists were able to blend by their imagination, which must be given as free a rein as the emotions. Imagination fuses and integrates the natural and supernatural, the conscious and unconscious, sign and symbol, fact and myth, physical and spiritual, man and animal. Reason discovers the breach; the intuitive imagination heals it. Since man himself is a symbol of nature, then his own intuitive imagination can apprehend the spiritual force back of the visible world. Since man is the finite containing a bit of the infinite, he is capable of breaking through physical boundaries to attain the spiritual. Man is still an integral part of nature and earth and tied as if by an umbilical cord to the inner life of the universe. Because of this innate union, he has the urge and capacity to penetrate into the earth's mysteries.

Coleridge recognized the imagination as the shaping spirit and the true inward creatrix. He described the poet as bringing all aspects of man into play, subordinating all faculties according to their relative worth and dignity. Imagination is the power which fuses them into a harmonious whole: ". . . Good sense is the Body of poetic genius, Fancy its Drapery, Motion its Life, and Imagination the Soul that is everywhere, and in each; and forms all into one graceful and intelligent whole."[12] Tracing Coleridge's water snakes in *The Rime of the Ancient Mariner* back to their literary birth, John Livingston Lowes stressed not the sources but the imaginative transformation they underwent in the mind of Coleridge and felt sure that the direction and movement which the raw materials took were more important than their original condition. Ugly phenomena became beautiful when subjected to the power of imagination:

> . . . the emphasis lies on the raw materials solely in their relation to the new whole which has been wrought from them. For their ultimate unity is not . . . without descent. And the recognition of its possibly dubious lineage simply heightens the glory of its latter state. In movement direction is everything, and the amazing fact is not that there was once a time "when mind was mud," but rather that mud in due course mounts to mind, and alligators and idiots and slimy seas become the stuff that dreams are made

on. That, I suspect, is one of the most momentous functions of the imagination—its sublimation of brute fact.[13]

Coleridge spoke of the "streamy nature of the associative faculty," which emerges from a deep well of chaotic images. When these associated ideas reach the top of the well, imagination, the "shaping spirit," begins to curb and rudder. Imagination is at work constantly seeking beauty.

Keats, too, recognized the directing power of imagination. In a letter to Benjamin Bailey, in which he repeats his thoughts on poetry as he had earlier expressed them to his brother George, Keats speaks of Fancy as the sails and "Imagination the Rudder."[14] In *Ode on a Grecian Urn,* the poet praises imagination: "Heard melodies are sweet, but those unheard / Are sweeter...."[15] Sensation, according to Keats, takes on a heightened value when idealized by the imagination.

Shelley, no less enthusiastically than Coleridge and Keats, praised the power of imagination:

> In a dramatic composition the imagery and the passion should interpenetrate one another, the former being reserved simply for the full development and illustration of the latter. Imagination is as the immortal God which should assume flesh for the redemption of mortal passion. It is thus that the most remote and the most familiar imagery may alike be fit for dramatic purposes when employed in the illustration of strong feeling, which raises what is low, and levels to the apprehension that which is lofty, casting over all the shadow of its own greatness.[16]

Such emphasis on the power of the imagination results in extravagant thought, emotion, and expression, which in turn frequently evoke much misunderstanding and abuse. Few movements have been so misunderstood and mutilated as Romanticism. No movement has been so vastly significant and sweeping in design, yet so evasive of definition. Even today, confusion still reigns:

> Collegiate philosophers still haggle over the beginnings of romanticism, the nature of romanticism, the destiny of

romanticism, each prodding a personal predilection. One blames Kant, another exalts Fenelon, one declares Bacon, another maintains Plato, and one asserts the Serpent, as the founder of Romanticism.[17]

It is interesting to think of the serpent as the founder of Romanticism. However disrespectful it may seem to call the serpent the predecessor of the Romanticists, the idea becomes less shocking when one remembers that Byron called Shelley the "snake" and that Shelley spoke of himself as the serpent who had been shut out of Paradise when he had to stop visiting Jane and Edward Williams, possibly as a result of Mary's objections to his attentions to Jane. Whether or not the relationship will bear a genealogical study, there are some parallels between the serpent and the Romanticists. The serpent instigated a revolt in the Garden of Eden by making Eve aware of her own individual needs and desires, of the pleasure in exercising one's choice instead of blindly obeying the decree of another, and of the joy in rejecting tradition and precedent to create one's own rules of behavior. Like the serpent, the Romanticists stressed individuality, vented their own thoughts and emotions, prevailed upon the rest of the world to do the same, rejected the decrees of the eighteenth century, and in general revolted against everything except the right to revolt.

No literary movement has lent itself to a greater expression of symbolism than Romanticism; no animal has lent itself to more symbolical interpretation than the serpent.

# II

## The Serpent and Romanticism

WHETHER THE SERPENT is the "founder of Romanticism" is questionable, but nevertheless it is an interesting suggestion. Little research is required, however, to discover the profound influence the serpent has had on the thoughts and literature of all people since the beginning of time. At times the snake is regarded as sacred, at other times as profane, or sometimes as an object evoking both reverence and hatred, but the snake is rarely considered just an ordinary animal pursuing its own way of existence with no significance for man. A survey of the Romantic movement quickly reveals that the Romanticists were fascinated by the serpent and were interested in its symbolic and imaginative value. An examination of several prominent aspects of the Romantic period helps us to understand the serpent's major role.

A significant aspect of Romanticism is a revived feeling toward nature, a sensuous delight in color, form, sound, and motion.[1] Keats's poetry particularly reveals this sensuous delight in nature. An apostle of beauty, Keats, like the Greeks and their delight in the physical world, exercised his imagination to present the object, not merely to describe it. Because of his firm grasp on concrete objects, his poetry is sensuous. In addition to sensuousness achieved by vivid presentation of the external aspects of the object, his poetry reveals a sensuous quality created by his ability to submerge his own personality and to penetrate the character of the object. Keats believed that the true poet hides his identity and takes on the color, mood, and the character of the object under consideration. In other words, the poet is like a chameleon, who is himself

> the most unpoetical of any thing in existence; because he has no Identity—he is continually informing and filling some other Body—The Sun, the Moon, the Sea, and Men and Women who are creatures of impulse are poetical and have about them an unchangeable attribute—the poet has none; no identity—he is certainly the most unpoetical of all God's Creatures.[2]

Among the various objects which Keats uses to create sensuousness and to evoke a physical, mental, and emotional reaction in the reader is the serpent, valuable for both its sensuous and sensual appeal. All of the major Romanticists, especially Shelley and Keats, stress the visual and kinesthetic appeal of objects. It is understandable, then, that the serpent with its color and muscular movement fascinated Shelley and Keats. Even though Wordsworth does not use the serpent extensively in his poetry, he creates many visual images which reveal his delight in a sense life and his readiness to receive impressions from the outer world. Byron's pleasure in witnessing and sharing the joys of nature does not derive so much from delight in exercising the senses as from the solace which nature as a refuge from unsympathetic society affords him. Hurt and eager for revenge, Byron finds the retaliatory nature of the serpent more interesting than its sensuous appeal. In addition to the use of the serpent for its sensuousness, Shelley stresses its symbolic value. Coleridge and Blake, too, find the psychological implications of the serpent of even more value than the physical.

However much the Romantic poets value the sense impression of nature, they stress even more the spiritual force energizing nature. In their moments of exercising the intuitive imagination, they discover within themselves a correspondence with the divinity pervading all the universe. Both the body and soul of man require sustenance, and nature possesses the nourishment for both. Dominance of the physical reduces man to a malevolent and ravaging serpent; dominance of the spiritual elevates man into a non-feeling ethereal wisp, unsuited for a mundane existence. The Romanticists regard the physical and spiritual as complements, and not necessarily as antagonists engaged in a deathlike struggle to achieve victory. Real victory lies within a reconciliation of the body and spirit. Man should not be like a serpent stretched out on the ground, feeling his way blindly about; neither should he be an unbodied spirit with no senses to delight in the pleasures of the physical world. The Romanticists, then, look to physical and divine nature as the model to follow in this integrating process.

The feeling that God, or an omnipresent spiritual force, resides in nature and that man himself is, like all other entities, an emanation of this divinity is called pantheism. Fundamental ideas at the base of the concept of pantheism are the adoration of Mother Earth, the senses of animal kinship, and the idea of reincarnation.

The adoration of Mother Earth grows out of the concept that God pervades all the earth and that the finiteness of even the serpent shares in the infiniteness of the all-pervading force just as the finiteness of man shares in this infiniteness. Thus, the Romanticists, intuiting God's infiniteness in the most finite forms of life, came to regard them with awe and love. Earth, the mother of all natural plant and animal life, is more powerful and ancient than all the gods. Mother Earth, in Shelley's *Prometheus Unbound,* expresses her superiority and impartiality as guardian of her creatures, all of which, including the "creeping forms," are her children, partaking of the same sustenance. The concept of animal kinship finds its most eloquent expression in man's recognition of the lowly and/or hateful serpent as sharing in the divinity pervading the universe. What more dramatic example of animal kinship can there be than the feeling of comradeship between man, erect in stature, and the serpent prone and crawling! An even greater expression of kinship is the transmigration of the human soul to the body of a serpent, the transformation of a serpent into a human being, or the transformation of a human being into a serpent. Mythology is replete with such legends.

Dissatisfied with the condition to which man had reduced himself, the Romanticists, like the mythological characters, found the

idea of relinquishing their human form for that of an animal or
plant desirable. The exercise of the intuitive imagination had
surmounted barriers between all forms of life and enabled man
to see that he, of all of God's creatures, had done the worst by
himself. Regretting man's separation from nature, the Romanticists began to contemplate the joys of losing their human forms
for those of a skylark, a nightingale, a leaf, a wave, or a cloud.
Shelley did not express a wish to be transformed into a snake,
but he does refer to himself as a snake in the poem *To Edward
Williams*. Byron was the first to call Shelley a "snake," specifically
in reference to his gliding in and out of rooms almost impercep-
tibly. It may also be an indirect comment on the latter's revolutionary ideas about the freedom of man.

The Romanticist's intuitive imagination revealed to him a sense
of mystery in the universe and in man. He was aware that reason
and the conscious could not fathom this mystery; therefore, he
began to rely on the intuitive imagination for an understanding
of the mystery. Freeing himself from a preoccupation with the
immediate and actual, he nostalgically looked backward for a
glimpse of a better world. This better world included the mythological world, free of the corruption of human institutions and
of the greed and tyranny of priests and kings. The late eighteenth
and early nineteenth-century world was sordid with the horrors
of child labor, slave-trade atrocities, and Napoleonic wars.

The mythological world, in contrast, was a natural state; man
was still an integral part of plant, mineral, and other animal life.
But the eighteenth century had not appreciated the significance
of the mythological world; thus, the Romanticists set about to restore freshness and vigor to the earth:

> Mythology, which had been reduced to a merely decorative
> function, or rejected altogether by the Augustan poets, was
> rehabilitated. The Gods and daemons of poetic fancy be-
> came, in Shelley and Keats especially, the living incarna-
> tions of the forces of the subconscious world, whose existence
> psychology was just beginning to divine. Fundamentally,
> this process was a rediscovery and a transvaluation of re-
> ligious symbolism, though only in the work of Blake was
> this phenomenon explicit.[3]

The Romantic poets recognized the vast treasury of mythology as containing symbolic significance for the experience of all of mankind. Lamb was particularly aware of the close relationship between mythology and man's unconscious. He realized that the study of mythology is simply another way of man's understanding his own mind:

> Gorgons, and Hydras, and Chimaeras—dire stories of Celaeno and the Harpies—may reproduce themselves in the brain of superstition—but they were there before. They are transcripts, types—the archetypes are in us, and eternal.— These terrors—date beyond body—or, without the body, they would have been the same[4]

The fact that four of the five mythological creatures which Lamb mentions are serpents or possess serpent characteristics emphasizes the important role of the serpent not only in mythology but also in man's conscious and unconscious thinking.

The poetry of the Romantics brings out the underlying, archetypal significance of the ancient mythological symbols they are employing. These poets value the myths as symbols of man's unconscious state. By re-creating the myths, they enable man to fathom his unconscious drives and by understanding them achieve a reconciliation and integration. The myths of classical antiquity, which had become relatively meaningless by the eighteenth century, were re-created by Wordsworth, Keats, and Shelley and given new life and potency as well as high poetical values. The traditional view saw in both symbol and myth poetic metaphor for some rational idea or, in a pragmatic sense, a useful fiction. Symbol and myth, from the traditional view, had no truth of their own but were given some aspect of truth by reason of an analogy to something else. This allegorical interpretation was discarded by the Romantic School:

> In the view of the Romanticists, the creation of a myth was not due to an intentional act of an inspired individual, but was the natural and unintentional activity of the collective mind. . . . Symbol and Myth are not intended to give, in a veiled manner, information about something known otherwise, but they reveal the innermost nature of a people. They do not copy reality, but they are responses to reality.[5]

Keats recognized classic myths as symbols with which to present a vision of man and a new world. The poem *I Stood Tip-toe* expresses Keats's affirmation of the identity of nature, myth, and poetry. Keats, a natural mythmaker, brings mythology alive by re-creating the old myths and by giving them modern implications. Thomas Raysor observes that Keats's earlier verse employs myth as symbols of sensate joys but his later poetry employs myth more as a pattern of thought "so that in the completed work myth and personal philosophy are integrated, myth-making genius combining with earnest endeavor to know and explain essentials."[6]

Like Keats, Shelley has a unique genius for myth-making. The Romanticists do not use mythology as a mere poetic device but recognize it as embodying a reconciliation of the biological and mental worlds. They seize upon the myths as symbols for bridging the gap between the natural and supernatural worlds and for helping man to reintegrate within himself his spiritual and physical drives. In this way, mythology aids him to reintegrate with all other plant and animal life—equal sharers in the cosmic divinity. This reaching into the mythological past is the Romanticist's attempt to re-enter a primordial state and restore himself to his natural divinity.

Such faith in mythology and its embodying psychological elements so fascinating to man since the beginning of time accounts for the array of mythological characters which come alive in the poetry of the Romantics. A very close survey of the classical myths reveals the astounding role the serpent plays, sometimes as friend and sometimes as enemy, but always conceived of as significant. The serpent is one of the most popular animals in mythology.

Another interest heightening the role of the serpent during the period of Romanticism was animal magnetism. London air was filled with the subject matter at the time that Coleridge was attending school, and from the pronounced interest in the hypnotic eye as treated in his works, he must have given some credence to the subject of ocular fascination. Even the poet himself felt the power of his own eye, which could rivet the attention of the listener and render him oblivious to all other aspects of the charmer. Like the "glittering eye" of the ancient mariner, Coleridge's own eye could detain the guest and with a steady gaze captivate and mesmerize him. This intense interest in animal magnetism helps to explain the numerous allusions to hypnotic glances and fascination found in the poems designed by Coleridge and Wordsworth for *Lyrical Ballads* in 1798. Coleridge's plan to take the supernatural and treat it as if real was a narrower range than Wordsworth's design of throwing over the natural something of the supernatural:

> ... so far as his [Coleridge's] salient ideas are concerned he hardly goes beyond the province of animal magnetism; and the notion of "fixing," and then of sudden release, keeps getting the mastery over him after the fashion of a hobby bestriding its rider. Add to this conception of "fixing" the readily associated idea of a good or an evil will in the magnetizer, which may naturally extend to blessing, or cursing the person who is "fixed," and we have the dominant notions in *Three Graves, The Rime of the Ancient Mariner,* and *Christabel,* and much of the contemporary *Osorio.*[7]

Lowes discusses in *The Road to Xanadu* Coleridge's interest in animal magnetism, a subject engrossing him so much

> that he proposed (as usual!) to write a book on it. Nor (again as usual) was his preoccupation hidden from his friends. "He will begin," wrote Southey to his wife in 1817, with a touch of not unnatural asperity, "as he did when I last saw him, about Animal Magnetism, or some equally congruous subject, and go on from Dan to Beersheba in his endless loquacity." Carlyle, in his contemptuous and cruel sketch of June 24, 1824, refers to him as "a kind, good soul, full of religion and affection, and poetry and animal magnetism."[8]

The poetry of Keats, Byron, and Shelley also reveals an interest in the hypnotic power of the eye not only of the serpent but also of some evil human beings.

Associated with the renewed awareness of nature, the attempt to re-create a mythological world, and the interest in animal magnetism is the tendency of the Romanticists to stress the supernatural, Gothic, and strange. Man's intuitive imagination pushed back the boundaries of the natural world and entered a supernatural world, full of wonder, strangeness, and grotesqueness. Even though the reason, senses, and consciousness cannot apprehend the supernatural world, it is foolish, according to the Romanticists, to deny these manifestations. Although a Victorian in time, Charles Gould is a true Romanticist in spirit when he expresses his willingness to believe in the existence of sea serpents. In *Mythical Monsters*,[9] Gould quotes Montaigne to support his belief that however incredible a thing may seem to man's reason it is extremely presumptuous to suppose that God and nature's power is limited by man's understanding. Montaigne's insistence that man avoid rejecting as incredible that which his limited mind and reason cannot affirm suggests Coleridge's tone in the description of his own contribution to *Lyrical Ballads*, done in collaboration with Wordsworth. Coleridge feels that his

> endeavors should be directed to persons and characters supernatural, or at least romantic; yet so as to transfer from our inward nature a human interest and a semblance of truth sufficient to procure for these shadows of imagination that willing suspension of disbelief for the moment, which constitutes poetic faith.[10]

The true Romantic finds the mythical world with all of its wonder, strangeness, and grotesqueness corresponding more closely to the world of his unconscious than does the visible world surrounding him. The supernatural world corresponds to the unconscious; the natural world appeals only to the conscious.

Gothic propensities of Shelley's mind are revealed in the following incident: Shelley, Dr. John Polidori, Mary Shelley, and Claire Clairmont were reading ghost stories one evening. After Byron had begun reading Coleridge's *Christabel*, Shelley arose and ran out of the room. Byron and Dr. Polidori followed and found Shelley faint and disturbed. Upon recovering, he told them that as he listened to the description of Lady Geraldine he had a vision of eyes in the place of nipples in Mary's bosom. This Gothic propensity in Shelley's poetry yields many images of the strange, supernatural, and grotesque world. Frequently the appearance of the serpent lends to this Gothic atmosphere an effect achieved by a combination of the ugly and the beautiful.

This combination of the ugly and the beautiful is the basis of the Romanticists' theory of beauty. This theory is in accordance with Lessing's concept of poetry as enunciated in *Laokoon*. Distinguishing poetry from sculpture, which deals with space, reproduces only one moment, and thus must treat necessarily of beauty, Lessing declares that poetry is not subject to these limitations. Instead poetry deals with time, can present a series of actions, and has the whole gamut of expression at its command. All of nature is the province of poetry, which can treat not only of the beautiful and agreeable but also of the ugly and terrible. Romanticism, with its rebelliousness toward all inhibition, moderation, and restraint, is an extravagant expression of Lessing's theory. Beauty, then, for the Romanticists is closely allied to suffering and agony. The horrid became an essential element of Romanticism and was a source of both beauty and poetry. It is true that the horrible causes pain, but for the Romanticists, pleasure grows out of this pain and is inseparable from it. The agony arising from the repulsive is a romantic one, and suffering is desirable. Accursed beauty, as is represented by the death-dealing, snaky-haired Medusa, is the supreme beauty:

> In fact, to such an extent were Beauty and Death looked upon as sisters by the Romantics that they became fused into a sort of two-faced herm, filled with corruption and melancholy and fatal in its beauty—a beauty which, the more bitter the taste, the more abundant the enjoyment.[11]

Shelley's poem *On the Medusa of Leonardo da Vinci in the Florentine Gallery* is an expression, or perhaps a manifesto, of the concept of beauty peculiar to the Romantics:

> 'Tis the tempestuous loveliness of terror;
>     For from the serpents gleams a brazen glare
> Kindled by that inextricable error,
>     Which makes a thrilling vapour of the air
> Become a ————— and ever-shifting mirror
>     Of all the beauty and the terror there—

> A woman's countenance, with serpent-locks,
> Gazing in death on Heaven from those wet rocks.[12]

Contemplating the picture of the serpent-haired Medusa, Shelley feels that the greatest beauty must emerge in combination with the horrible. The influence of the Medusa is not attributable just to her loveliness but to the combination of her beauty subjected to the agony caused by the vipers wreathing her face. Beauty is most powerful when it evokes the greatest emotion, and the most intense emotions are those growing out of suffering. This same habit of looking for beauty in ugliness carries over to Shelley's search for goodness in badness. Illustrating the poet's belief that the apparent is not always what it seems is his use of the generally scorned serpent to symbolize beauty, truth, or goodness.

Kenneth Burke observes that the idea of "beauty" became obscured in the nineteenth century because the aesthetic theorists, who were comfortable and at leisure, stressed the decorative rather than the sublime. But the very fact that poetry seeks to stress the beautiful implies the need for protection against ugliness. In other words, poetry is produced for purposes of comfort, and in order to analyze the element of comfort in beauty, continues Burke, we must examine the element of discomfort, for which the poetry is "medicine." Thus, threat becomes the basis of beauty. That the Romanticists used the serpent as a threat out of which beauty may emerge, or that the word "serpent" or the animal itself is used to compare human beings, their actions, and areas of life and experience, is supported by abundant images and symbolic episodes:

> ... we see Coleridge, among the greatest critics of world literature, likening the work of Shakespeare to the movements of a serpent, while in "The Ancient Mariner," a poem explicitly of fascination and terror, we have that fatal moment of recreation when the loathsome watersnakes are proclaimed blessed and beautiful.[13]

To the Romanticists no basic contradiction existed between the ugly and the beautiful. Both often stir the emotions, an experience which the Romanticists found desirable.

The power of the intuitive imagination of the Romanticists reconciles the irreconcilables—body and spirit, nature and the supernatural, the conscious and unconscious, ugliness and beauty, badness and goodness, and falseness and truth. And the serpent in the poetry of the Romanticists is the best animal image and symbol for analyzing, comparing, and synthesizing these irreconcilables.

# III

## Serpent Imagery in the Major Romantics

For PURPOSES OF CRITICAL ANALYSIS, serpent images in the poetry of the major Romanticists—Blake, Wordsworth, Coleridge, Byron, Shelley, and Keats—can be broken down into six classifications: those comparing man's emotions with the serpent; those comparing his physical and mental attributes with the serpent; those comparing the whole man with the serpent; those comparing areas and aspects of human life and experiences with the serpent; those comparing natural phenomena and man-made objects with the serpent; and those in which the serpent is presented as mere animal or as pictorial detail.

The serpent images of the first five classifications are generally expressed in metaphors and similes. The last classification does not use the serpent for comparison but only for description of a phenomenalistic world.

A breakdown of the images in the first three classifications is difficult to make in that the images overlap to some extent and some can conceivably fit into all three categories. Even though the breakdown is somewhat arbitrary and some of the images seem to fit into possibly all three categories, they are placed in their more natural and, thus, primary classification.

The fourth classification of images compares areas and aspects of human life and experiences with the serpent and presents man in his relation to other men and to God. In other words, these images deal with man in a social and spiritual context. The first four classifications, then, proceed from aspects of man to the whole man and finally to man in a context.

The fifth classification includes images in which natural phenomena and man-made objects are compared to a serpent. Because the Romanticists present man as copying or imitating nature in his productions, this grouping is useful and valid.

Images in the sixth classification present the serpent as mere animal and as vivid detail in a description of the phenomenalistic world. The serpent is not used to compare or describe man and his life but is presented as an inhabitant of a world appealing primarily to the senses.

It is necessary to stress at this point that the images are generally classified and treated for their descriptive, overt, obvious, and visible value. As nearly as possible, the images are analyzed in the light of what they state, not what they imply. The symbolic values in serpent imagery are discussed in the next chapter. A study of the symbolism requires an interpretative approach, an examination of what the image implies rather than what it states, a search for the latent rather than the obvious meaning, a grasping of the invisible rather than the visible, and a preoccupation with the covert rather than the overt. Serpent imagery only is discussed in the present chapter.

The inclusion and discussion of all the serpent images in all these classifications would have resulted in a formidable and complex mass of data. Therefore, representative images have been selected and are discussed rather fully. The other images are referred to in the notes. The images discussed are chosen for their originality and general effectiveness of idea or expression or of both. Some of them are particularly thought-provoking and stimulating. Others are dramatic, expressive, and forceful. The criteria, then, for selection and discussion of the images are originality and creativity of thought and/or expression, as opposed to popularity and conventionality.

For compactness and ease in contrasting and comparing the poets' uses of the serpent, all representative images falling into the same classification are discussed consecutively. In other words, the six poets are taken up chronologically. For example, all serpent images describing emotions are presented and discussed, beginning with Blake, continuing with Wordsworth, Coleridge, Byron, Shelley, and ending with Keats. This order is followed throughout the presentation of the selected images in all other classifications as well. Mention will be made wherever any poet does not have an image fitting the particular classification under discussion.

## Man's Emotions

Serpent images describing the emotions are chosen because they reveal something of the essence and temperament of Romanticism and of the poets themselves. It is not surprising that the Romantics, aware of man's sensuous and sensual nature, should find the serpent so helpful in describing emotions, passions, and feelings. The poisonous viper is especially valuable to the Romanticists in their descriptions of those physical and mental conditions which contribute to man's disintegration.

Blake's poetry is so highly symbolical that it is almost impossible to treat of the images in a meaningful way without some consideration of the symbolism. This consideration makes it possible to choose the following image as representative of Blake's comparison of lust or sexual desire to a serpent. Urizen (Reason) prepares for war against Orc (Revolution), who in his human and, thus, divine form rebels against Urizen's repressive forces. Urizen sends Vala, his harlot, to calm Orc:

> So Orc roll'd round his clouds upon the deeps of
>     dark Urthona,
> Knowing the arts of Urizen were Pity & Meek affection
> And that by these arts the serpent form exuded from
>     his limbs
> Silent as despairing love & strong as jealousy,
> Jealous that she was Vala, now become Urizen's Harlot
> And the Harlot of Los & the deluded harlot of the
>     Kings of the Earth,
> His soul was gnawn in sunder.[1]

Orc in his human and divine form rolls around on the clouds in the realm of Urthona, representing spiritual energy, one of the Four Zoas or Four Senses, which when in harmony develop the Eternal Man. Having warred for control of man, the Four Zoas or Four Senses are now residing in their own individual realms of the world of time and space. Vala finds Orc in Urthona's realm, which is deep, dark, and isolated. In her effort to mitigate Orc's fury, Vala expresses pity and meek affection or love. Even though Orc recognizes these assumed qualities as arts taught to her by Urizen, he is at the same time weakened by them. Desirous of Vala, he is jealous that she is the harlot of Urizen, Los, and other self-appointed kings on earth—all of whom have rejected divinity and unity for their own material world. Feeling himself vulnerable to the temptations of Vala and her lords, Orc identifies his lust with a serpent. However, he must not manifest his lust in violent actions but let it exude from his limbs as quietly as a hopeless love, even though it has the strength of jealousy. The conflict between desire for the attractions of Urizen's material world, on one hand, and resistance to his repressive forces, on the other, is so intense that Orc's soul is torn asunder.

Wordsworth uses the viper in a rather traditional manner when he compares a lover's remorse for his errors to the stings of a viper. Pushed into defiance of unfair laws which separated him from his loved one, a youth suffered and lay passively until remorse, like the stings of a viper, stirred him from his couch. Deploring man's unnatural laws which forced the youth into rebellion and greater crimes, Wordsworth illustrates in a tale the unhappiness arising from such conditions. The reader may learn

> how the enamoured youth was driven,
> By public power abased, to fatal crime,
> Nature's rebellion against monstrous law;
> How, between heart and heart, oppression thrust
> Her mandates, severing whom true love had joined,
> Harassing both; until he sank and pressed
> The couch his fate had made for him; supine,
> Save when the stings of viperous remorse,
> Trying their strength, enforced him to start up,
> Aghast and prayerless.[2]

These thoughts are in lamentation of the inhumanity abroad in France at the time of the French Revolution. Like all the other Romantic poets, Wordsworth stressed the rights of the individual and was aware of the suffering growing out of neglect of them.

The mind of man is the glory of the world. Man is worthy of himself only when he realizes the dignity and power of which his mind is capable, owing to his essentially human endowment. This power is the fundamental assertion of the mind itself, genuine liberty, the full exercise of which is moral freedom and happiness. When deprived of this exercise of liberty, the individual is likely to rebel against unfair laws and, thus, become the victim of even greater suffering. The misfortune of the enamored youth exemplifies the evil which results when law takes precedence over the inherent rights of the individual.

Coleridge's image in which the child PAIN lifts his snaky scourge in vengeance against his mother ERROR is powerful and moving. According to the poet, the noblest province of man is

> To rear some realm with patient discipline,
> Aye bidding PAIN, dark ERROR's uncouth child,
> Blameless Parenticide! his snakey scourge
> Lift fierce against his Mother![3]

The poet envisions a wonderful kingdom arising from the strength, patience, and discipline of a race of people who refuse to let their mistakes and suffering enervate and destroy them. Coleridge may be associating error with understanding, which he and the other Romantics felt is inadequate in grasping truth. Man's reliance upon the senses and the faculty of understanding results in experience only, not truth, and leaves man disillusioned and hurt. ERROR, fumbling in the dark, gives birth to PAIN; understanding, incapable of finding its way through the shadow world of reality to the clear, light world of ideality, leads human nature to ruin. How commendable that a nation would recognize its mistakes and take up arms against them rather than become cowed and destroyed by them. ERROR, causing much misery, should be treated like an unfeeling and unconscientious mother, who deserves punishment at the hands of her child, made uncouth and disobedient through suffering and mistreatment. PAIN, like the abused child, knows no filial love for ERROR, who is responsible for its misery, and like a bludgeoned child is justified in killing its parent ERROR with a vengeance as violent as that of the snaky-haired Gorgons. For greatest effectiveness and full impact, the image should be read aloud. The labored phrasing, awkward syntax, and harsh sounds reinforce the violence of the idea of a child's revenge against his parent or of PAIN's scourging with snakes its mother ERROR.

A self-admitted "fool of passion," Byron reveals something of his temperament in an image in which man's passions are described as serpents finding their way to the liver, where they lodge and thrive. Anatomizing the body and explaining philosophically the physiological functions of its parts, the poet traces all mischief to man's liver, which he labels as a lazaret or storehouse:

> The liver is the lazaret of bile,
> But very rarely executes its function,
> For the first passion stays there such a while,
> That all the rest creep in and form a junction,
> Life [Like] knots of vipers on a dunghill's soil,—
> Rage, fear, hate, jealousy, revenge, compunction,—
> So that all mischiefs spring up from this entrail,
> Like earthquakes from the hidden fire called "central."[4]

The liver fails to function properly in releasing its storage of bile for causing important changes in the blood stream necessary for man's good health. Taking advantage of this physical weakness, the first passion makes its way to the liver and establishes a lodging, thus turning the liver into a lazaret, where all other passions like diseased and impoverished lepers creep in and live, thriving in the darkness, dampness, stagnation, and foulness just as vipers thrive in the soil of a dunghill. These passions—rage, fear, hate, jealousy, revenge, compunction—are squirming knots of vipers, all in junction to secure control of man, but in their struggle to achieve dominance fight among themselves, inciting man to outward manifestations which Byron compares to earthquakes whose source is a raging fire hidden deep within the earth.

Even though the snake-eagle image is a conventional one and appears several times in Shelley's poetry, he makes an original and effective use of it in *Alastor*, where he describes a frustrated lover and his attempts to find his loved one. The mad pursuit of the lover, probably Shelley himself, driven by an anguished

desire for the veiled Lady, Ideal Love, is no less frenzied than
the precipitous flight of an eagle in escaping from the poisonous
folds of a serpent:

> As an eagle grasped
> In folds of the green serpent, feels her breast
> Burn with the poison, and precipitates
> Through night and day, tempest, and calm, and cloud,
> Frantic with dizzying anguish, her blind flight
> O'er the wide aery wilderness: thus driven
> By the bright shadow of that lovely dream,
> Beneath the cold glare of the desolate night,
> Through tangled swamps and deep precipitous dells,
> Starting with careless step the moonlight snake,
> He fled.[5]

The reader immediately interprets the simile as a comparison of
the lover with the eagle and of the veiled lady with the serpent.
However, this analogy breaks down when one discovers that the
eagle and the lover are fleeing in opposite directions. The eagle
tries frantically to escape the serpent's constricting and poisonous
folds and, thus, catapults through space away from the serpent.
The lover, on the other hand, tries frantically to go toward the
veiled lady and be enveloped by her arms. Another point of contrast is that the paralyzing and poisonous folds of the serpent are
offensive to the eagle; whereas, the embracing arms of the veiled
lady and their power to inflame the lover's breast are desirable.
Therefore, the analogy lies not between the eagle and the
serpent, on one hand, and the lover and the veiled lady, on the
other, but between the serpent's poison and its effect on the
eagle, and anguished desire and its effect on the lover. The
serpent's poison burns the eagle's breast so painfully that the
eagle catapults through the heavens; desire for the veiled lady
burns the lover's breast so consumingly that he dashes madly
and erratically about in pursuit of her. Poisoned with anguished
desire, the lover behaves in the same frantic manner as the eagle
poisoned by the serpent.

Shelley's use of green as the color of the snake intensifies its
poisoning power and suggests the lover's jealousy and possessive-

ness, which blind his reason and lead him carelessly through tangled swamps and precipitous dells. Another bit of evidence to indicate that the analogy lies between poison and its effect on the eagle and anguished desire and its effect on the lover is Shelley's use of the pronoun "her" to refer to the eagle. If the poet had intended the comparison of the eagle and lover, he might have used the masculine gender "his." Even though the use of the pronoun "her" avoids this problem, it produces another in that it creates a conflict for the reader by momentarily tricking him into a temptation to equate the eagle with the veiled lady, or Ideal Love, who scorns the ground and contact with all earthly life and soars as does the eagle in an effort to escape the serpent. Tempting as it might be to compare the eagle and the lover or the eagle and the veiled lady, the complete image will not sustain either analogy but instead restricts the comparison to a simple but effective equation of poison and its effect on the eagle with anguished desire and its effect on the lover. Presumptuousness dares to suggest that an eagle of no gender would have been more consonant with the total concept of the image. Sexualization is more effective when left to the imagination of the individual, who is then free to project, identify, or empathize his own feelings.

Emphasizing the sensuous quality of poetry, Keats found the muscular movement of the serpent fascinating. Comparison of agony and other enervating emotions to a serpent is a conventional image in the poetry of the Romantics, but one to which Keats adds a refreshing touch. The poet succeeds in using the serpent to describe both the emotional and physical states. The body, under the control of transforming serpent-agony, becomes a serpent, too. Such complete subjection of the physical to the emotional results in a stimulating image. Hyperion, incensed at and suffering from the ejection of Saturn and the Titans from Mt. Olympus, resolves to reinstate his leader:

> . . . through all his bulk an agony
> Crept gradual, from the feet unto the crown,
> Like a lithe serpent vast and muscular
> Making slow way with head and neck convuls'd
> From over-strained might.[6]

Frequently the Romantic poets describe emotions, passions, or feelings as serpents wreathed about the head proclaiming man's guilt, entwined around and stifling the heart, wrapped about the body in constricting and paralyzing folds, or insidiously secreted in some concealed part of the body, where they torture and ener-vate man into a bestial condition without pride, care, or self-re-spect. In Keats's image, agony is a large, angry serpent straining and pushing itself forward, tensing and swelling its neck and head in effort, transforming Hyperion's bulky body into a long, lithe serpent muscling itself from feet to head in fierce determination. Thus, Keats's presentation of agony as a serpent forcing its way through the entire length of Hyperion's body and, thereby, evok-ing a physical reaction mirroring his emotional state is vivid and forceful.

## Man's Physical and Mental Attributes

Serpent images are found in the description of the specific mental and physical attributes of reason, cogitations, thoughts, a frown, conscience, breath, and a glance. Even though compari-son of these attributes with a serpent is rather familiar, the Ro-mantic poets strip away the familiarity and reveal many exciting, strange, and sometimes startling ideas.

Blake sees thought, or analytic reason, transforming the infinite into a serpent, an image discussed later in areas and aspects of human life and experience. Reason not only has the power to change other things into serpents; it is itself a serpent, constrict-ing and paralyzing man. Seeing Albion lying cold and in a death-like sleep induced by the dulling and deadening effects of reason, which haunts like a spectre, Blake pleads for help to free Albion:

> O Divine Spirit! sustain me on thy wings,
> That I may awake Albion from his long & cold repose!
> For Bacon & Newton, sheath'd in dismal steel, their
>     terrors hang
> Like iron scourges over Albion. Reasonings like vast
>     serpents
> Infold around my limbs, bruising my minute articu-
>     lations.[7]

The poet conceives of the Divine Spirit as having wings and floating above the earth, but sees serpent-reason grounded to the earth, where it in turn grounds man. Albion lies stretched out in a sleep of stupor, forced to remain there because the errors of Bacon's inductive philosophy and Newton's mathematical demonstrations are poised above his body like cold, drab steel ready to assault him should he move. Knowing himself vulnerable to the constrictions and scourges of the same serpent-reason, the poet appeals to the Divine Spirit to support him on its wings while he tries to awaken Albion and free him from the paralysis induced by serpent-reason. The spirit cut off from divinity, the poet agonizes in the coils of serpent-reason and in this state cannot apprehend truth and give it accurate and complete expression. Serpent-reason is mechanical, imperfect, and analytical; the intuitive imagination is spontaneous, perfect, and synthetical. Serpent-reason fetters; imagination frees.

Stressing a spiritual and mental life, Wordsworth builds a reflective image on a war-worn chieftain, who quits the world to go into seclusion, where his cogitations, like ivy, bind him in serpentine strictures:

> . . . within his cell,
> Round the decaying trunk of human pride,
> At morn, and eve, and midnight's silent hour,
> Do penitential cogitations cling;
> Like ivy, round some ancient elm, they twine
> In grisly folds and strictures serpentine.[8]

The warrior relinquishes a physical, energetic, and active life for a spiritual and mental one. Lance, sword, and shield are put aside. Hands empty, thoughts fill the mind. Youth is spent in action; age is spent reflecting on and evaluating those actions. Retreating from the battlefield, the arena for the body's expression, the weary chieftain seeks the quietness and privacy of the forest depths or the cloister, where in penitence his thoughts dwell on the futility of war, vanity of life, and fragility of body. The chieftain, old and unproductive in body, is like an old elm tree. Past fruition, both stiffen and solidify into supports, around which thoughts and ivy cling. These thoughts, once hard and aggressive but now soft and penitent, are profuse and clinging like ivy and wrap themselves into convolute, constricting, and serpentine folds about man. The body wasted, the mind controls. The thoughts are no longer dynamic, enterprising, and progressive but are static, fixed, and retrogressive. Life in cloistered privacy permits no new experiences but only a reflection on the past. Life for the old warrior is contemplation without action; existence for the old elm is vegetation without fruition. Even though thoughts and ivy bind and restrict like serpents, they bring a reward in that both provide their own bower to which man can retreat to reflect on and spiritualize his actions and experiences.

In a completely different vein, Coleridge banishes thoughts, which he, too, compares to serpents coiling around his mind. The poet laments the loss of the faculty of response from within to the beauty of the natural world and of that "shaping spirit of Imagination" which nature gave him at birth. Thoughts as vipers coiling about the mind constitute a typical Romantic protest against a world impoverished by reason, which, because limited, perceives only the physical world, a shadow—a dark dream—of the ideal world lying beyond, penetrable only by the intuitive imagination. Realizing his impoverished condition and striving to recapture the spell of nature, he commands: "Hence, viper thoughts, that coil around my mind,/Reality's dark dream!"[9] Bowed by afflictions, the poet cares not that they have robbed him of his mirth but despairs that each visitation dulls his most precious faculty, the imagination, nature's gift. However dull and stifling life may be, imagination enables man to transcend these limitations of the physical world and to catch glimpses of the spiritual world. Afflictions force upon man an awareness of the body enclosed and constricted by reality. With the mind subordinated to the body, man's imagination is stifled by earth-bound thoughts. Man's tendency to reason and to destroy with the meddling intellect is like a serpent which constricts and strangles his intuitive imaginative power.

Byron's image deals with the hypnotic power of the serpent's eye rather than its ability to constrict and strangle. In the beginning of the nineteenth century, Greece was involved in a fierce struggle for independence. Byron's love for Greece rendered him helplessly vulnerable to her suffering. Any frown or expression of pain or grief was unbearable to the sympathetic poet and was as paralyzing to him as the adder's eye to its victim, the frail bird. Proud, indomitable, arrogant, and revengeful, Byron and his Byronic heroes generally pride themselves on being like serpents, stinging only when stung and inspiring fear and awe in their offenders. So when in the following image the poet plays the role of a poor bird paralyzed into complete submission and at the mercy of the adder's hypnotic eye, the reversal provides a stimulating contrast which verges on being humorous, provided one can forget the seriousness of his love for Greece even to the extent of losing his life in her struggle for independence. The poet confesses:

> I am a fool of passion, and a frown
> > Of thine to me is an adder's eye.
> To the poor bird whose pinion fluttering down
> > Wafts unto death the breast it bore so high;
> Such is this maddening fascination grown,
> > So strong thy magic or so weak am I.[10]

His love for Greece is so great that with her smile the poet can soar to great heights but with her frown he falls limply to the ground. He is like a poor bird hypnotized into helplessness by the adder's magic gaze. Its wings, which carry the bird to great heights, now flap and beat in much agitation but without transporting it. Under the spell of the serpent's eye, the bird, unable to fly to safety, falls to the ground, where death awaits it. The poet's love for Greece has turned into a fascination, devoid of all reason and sense. Thus, when the beloved country frowns, he too is helpless, whether from her power to fascinate him or from his own weakness. The poet's passion may be equated with the bird's pinion: both enable their possessors to soar to great heights, on one hand, but, on the other, losing their control waft them to an equal depth. Byron's confession that he is "a fool of passion" may very well be a terse but laconic creed of all the Romantic poets, stressing the importance of feeling in a phenomenalistic world of many sensuous pleasures, yet realizing that passion in excess renders man twice victimized—by the object inspiring the passion and by the passion itself.

An effective illustration of the images dealing with man's physical and mental attributes is Shelley's comparison of a relentless conscience to a serpent. Queen Mab has rescued the Spirit of Ianthe from the body's grave and taken her to an ethereal home above the earth. Looking down at the world of man as she speaks to Ianthe, Queen Mab enumerates the evils which plague and weaken man. Among these evils is his emphasis on pride, wealth, power, and custom. Expressing Shelley's views, Queen Mab is scornful of the king whose efforts to appease an insatiable appetite enslave his poor subjects. Having eaten and drunk himself into a stupor, the king lies sleeping on a gorgeous couch until

> "conscience, that undying serpent,
>         calls
> Her venomous brood to their nocturnal task."[11]

Conscience and her brood cause the king so much agony that he prays for the peace which accompanies poverty.

Keats's rather heavy reliance on classical mythology may explain in part the conventionality of many of the serpent images in his poetry. Keats and the other Romantic poets steeped in mythology appear to have been fascinated by the cockatrice or basilisk. This mythical creature is said to be hatched by a reptile from a cock's egg and is represented as killing its victim, at times by emitting a deadly vapor, and at others by casting a fatal glance. This power which made the basilisk or cockatrice a formidable foe was rendered ineffective, however, if the intended victim saw it first. In *Otho the Great,* Ludolph finds himself in this advantageous position. Instead of succumbing to Albert's fatal glance, Ludolph, knowing that he has caught the other's evil eye first and thereby rendered it ineffective, gloats in his reproach of Albert:

> O Cockatrice,
> I have you. Whither wander those fair eyes
> To entice the Devil to your help ... ?[12]

Ethelbert, a character in the same drama, is also aware of the power of the cockatrice. He queries of himself why he hesitates to reveal the names of Auranthe and Conrad, whom he calls vipers because of their venomous action against Princess Erminia:

> Yet why do I delay to spread abroad
> The name of those two vipers from whose jaws
> A deadly breath went forth to taint and blast
> This guileless lady?[13]

Even though Ethelbert does not call them basilisks or cockatrices, he implies this identification by attributing to them a breath which tainted and blasted a lady's innocence. Ability to kill one's victim with a single glance of the eye or a blast of the breath is an enviable power when one finds himself cornered with his foe. However unoriginal in presentation, the idea of such power at one's command is inherently captivating to all persons, each of whom at some time in life imagines or wishes himself capable of vanquishing his foe with one masterful and irrevocable gesture.

## The Whole Man

The Romantic poets frequently portray the whole nature of man as viperous; or if not viperous by nature, he is caught up in a circumstance transforming him into a snake, or feels himself born into a world of paltry conditions which make his lot no better than that of reptiles. Stressing the necessity of individual freedom, the Romantics often equate with snakes all foes of liberty, particularly tyrants, kings, and priests, who plague and penalize men with restraints and restrictions. Other human beings who in some way are blemishes upon the earth are also compared to serpents.

The serpent in Blake's imagery plays a major and exciting role. One of the poet's common themes is man's loss of divinity. Because for Blake the human and the divine forms are identical, man's separation from divinity results in a transformation from the human form to the serpent. Thus, when Orc falls under the power of Urizen in his creation of a world of time and space as opposed to an eternal world, he becomes a serpent valuing only the material world for its sensuous appeal. Preparing for war initiated by Jesus in an attempt to regenerate man, Urizen observes that Orc is changing into a serpent and is among his allies:

> ... for Orc augmented swift
> In fury, a Serpent wondrous, among the Constellations
>     of Urizen.
> A crest of fire rose on his forehead, red as the
>     carbuncle;
> Beneath, down to his eyelids, scales of pearl;
>     then gold & silver,
> Immingled with the ruby, overspread his Visage; down
> His furious neck, writhing contortive in dire budding
>     pains,
> The scaly armour shot out. Stubborn down his back &
>     bosom,
> The Emerald, Onyx, Sapphire, jasper, beryl, amethyst
> Strove in terrific emulation which should gain a
>     place
> Upon the mighty Fiend—the fruit of the mysterious
>     tree
> Kneaded in Uveth's kneading trough. Still Orc devour'd
>     the food
> In raging hunger. Still the pestilential food in gems
>     & gold
> Exuded around his awful limbs, Stretching to serpent
>     length
> His human bulk, While the dark shadowy female,
>     brooding over,
> Measur'd his food, morning & evening in cups & baskets
>     of iron.[14]

The atmosphere is tense and fraught with color, movement, fury, pain, and greed. The image is a riot of color—red, pearl, gold, silver, ruby, green, black, blue, yellow, brown, and purple—each vying to outdo the others. The words and phrases "augmented swift," "rose," "overspread," "shot out," and "strove" characterize the movement as violent, sudden, and competitive. The "neck, writhing contortive in dire budding pains" lends to the effect of struggle and suffering. The gems stubbornly striving "in terrific emulation" repeat the theme of conflict and intensify the struggle. Just as Urizen and Orc fight for the preservation of their position in the material world, so the gems strive for an enviable position among the material splendor of Orc's body. The phrase "red as the carbuncle" is rich in denotative and connotative meanings of color, stone, and pain. The pearl, gold, silver, ruby, emerald, onyx, sapphire, jasper, beryl, and amethyst are not only the attire in which Urizen dresses Orc as a convert to the material world but also food for his voracious appetite.

Only a trough is large enough to hold food for Orc's insatiate appetite, whetted by the material world. Here, Uveth, daughter of Urizen, kneads the fruit taken from her father's tree. Stretching his serpent-length along the ground, Orc devours the food until it exudes from his body. Thus, his insatiable appetite has converted his whole body into the food it craves so much. "The dark shadowy female," a handmaiden in the service of Urizen, measures Orc's food in cups and baskets, which are made of iron as inflexible and unyielding as the reason of Urizen. Only baskets are suitable for serving large quantities of food to a ravenous serpent. The word "brooding" further characterizes the reluctance of "the dark shadowy female" to execute a task which Urizen's daughters have assigned to her.

Wordsworth makes an interesting use of Hercules' experience with the snakes surrounding his cradle to describe France's experience with her foes:

> . . . the Invaders fared as they deserved:
> The Herculean Commonwealth had put forth
> her arms
> And throttled with an infant godhead's might
> The snakes about her cradle.[15]

Before Hercules was a year old, he revealed his greatness of soul and strength in the face of danger. Furious that Alcmena bore Hercules to Zeus, Hera, determined to kill the infant, began her revenge by sending two snakes crawling into the nursery where Hercules and his brother slept. The serpents, with weaving heads and flicking tongues, reared themselves over the cradle and

awoke the infants. Unlike Iphicles, who screamed and scrambled
to flee, Hercules grasped the serpents by the throat and killed
them even though they were entwined about his body. Such
bravery and strength characterized his entire life spent in defeat-
ing Hera's challenges. Love and sympathy for the youthful
France in her struggle for freedom suggested to the idealistic
Wordsworth the vast strength, unflinching courage, and supreme
self-confidence which rendered Hercules invulnerable to all
defeat except by the supernatural. Like the serpents who invaded
the nursery where Hercules slept, the reactionary powers of
Europe invaded France in 1792 and were joined by England in
1793. France, however, in 1802 defeated her enemies in her
struggle for establishing freedom and other popular liberties.
Under Napoleon, France had strangled the feudal strongholds
of Europe, if only temporarily. Thus, the Herculean Commonwealth had triumphed over the serpent invaders.

The Greeks' choice of a soulless butterfly to represent a soul
provides Coleridge with an interesting contrast between its lot,
which is delightful, and man's, which is reptile:

> The butterfly the ancient Grecians made
> The soul's fair emblem, and its only name—
> But of the soul, escaped the slavish trade
> Of mortal life!—For in this earthly frame
> Ours is the reptile's lot, much toil, much blame,
> Manifold motions making little speed,
> And to deform and kill the things whereon we feed.[16]

It is ironical that the existence of the butterfly, which has no soul,
is more pleasant than that of man, who has a soul. Lacking a
soul and free to flit and soar, the butterfly escapes the enslave-
ment to which man is subject. Man's soul is lodged in a body,
earthbound and impeded like the serpent's. He must crawl and
feel his way about, risking his life to the desires, demands, and
dislikes of others. Like the serpent whose many sinuous movements carry him short distances and with difficulty, man writhes,
advances, retreats, deviates, making a great stir but little progress.
He, too, like the serpent, incurs hatred and scorn. The butterfly

feeds on the pollen of plants and flowers, satisfying its needs but leaving no blemish; serpent and man, on the other hand, are predatory and must harm and destroy in order to eat. The poet seems to imply regret that man's physical frame, like the serpent's, is earthbound and enslaves him; he does not regret, however, that man has a soul. The sad thing is to have a body which subjects one's soul to conditions fit only for a reptile.

Byron, on the other hand, succeeds in making the reptile an almost enviable creature. Conrad, the Corsair, a typically Byronic hero with a consuming passion to wreak vengeance on an unsympathetic and hateful world, is like a serpent, whom man may hate but will treat with deference. Like the venomous snake, the Corsair may expire in the struggle but not before he has dealt his death sting:

> Man spurns the worm, but pauses ere he wake
> The slumbering venom of the folded snake:
> The first may turn, but not avenge the blow;
> The last expires, but leaves no living foe;
> Fast to the doom'd offender's form it clings,
> And he may crush—not conquer—still it stings![17]

With no fear of retaliation, man may contemptuously or carelessly crush the worm or thrust it to the side of the path, intent on pursuing his own way of life without interruption or hindrance. An unexpected worm at one's feet does not frighten or provoke but is impulsively and automatically brushed aside. Discovering the coiled serpent in his path, however, man is confronted with a danger which must be handled cautiously and with deference. The coils are a reservoir of potential power enabling the snake to strike farther. Within this reservoir is venom, which though slumbering is deadly. The worm may, by moving, show some annoyance at being disturbed but secures its life because it has no power to avenge; the snake, on the other hand, has the power to avenge the blow but loses its life. Expressed paradoxically, the worm's weakness is its strength; the snake's strength is its weakness. Man may crush the serpent but fails to conquer, in that the poisonous serpent while dying is still able to inflict reciprocal death on its offender. The worm lives, but its offender lives, too. Man conquers the worm without crushing but crushes the serpent without conquering. The Corsair, perhaps Byron himself, disdains life secured through weakness. Death demanding deference is more desirable than life begging for mercy. So it is with a degree of pride that the Corsair, and possibly Byron, identify themselves with the serpent, inspiring awe and demanding respect, rather than with the worm, soliciting only mercy.

One of the most effective images in which man himself is compared to the serpent or in some way is related to the serpent is that portraying kings and their vanity and despotism. An interesting observation is Shelley's apparent fascination with the association of king and sand. The king in his desire to perpetuate his name and deeds erects monuments of stone on the desert. In his determination to leave an impression on the world, he selects stone, which like himself is hard and unrelenting, possessing power to impress but with little capacity to receive impressions. The desert sand, on the other hand, is soft and yielding and is the most impressionable of elements. It is ironical, however, that the quality of sand which renders it impressionable also prevents its retaining impressions. Even more ironical is the fact that Ozymandias in his determination to leave a constant and permanent mark on the world would choose a foundation as shifting, inconstant, and impermanent as sand on which to erect stone monuments in tribute to himself. The poem *Ozymandias* illustrates effectively the contrast between the vanity of kings and the world's disregard of such vanity. The silence and undisturbed demeanor of the long stretches of sand into the distance express the desert sand's scorn for vanity's imperious demands. Although this poem contains no serpent imagery, it contributes to the idea that Shelley found the association of king, stone, and sand interesting and serves to heighten the effectiveness of the king-serpent-sand image in the following discussion.

Shelley denounces in the name of liberty even the name "king." His suggestion for the extinction of the word is that it be written lightly in the sand and thus be erased from the earth just as the serpent's trail vanishes when the air stirs:

> Oh, that the free would stamp the impious name
>    Of King into the dust! or write it there,
> So that this blot upon the page of fame
>    Were as a serpent's path, which the light air
> Erases, the flat sands close behind![18]

Since the poet conceives of a king as cold and creeping, it is particularly appropriate that he think of the name "king" written in the sand as sinuous and tenuous as the serpent's trail, which the faintest breath of air disperses, leveling the sand to a long and vacant stretch, unresponsive and blank.

Representing Keats's use of the serpent to depict man's whole nature is his image of the mythological Circe, a beguiling and bewitching woman of evil power. Glaucus tells Endymion how Circe enchanted him into forgetting Scylla, his ideal love. He portrays Circe as a malevolent snake, who charms and transforms man into a bestial condition. When Glaucus went to search for Circe, who had slipped from his side during sleep, he found her bewitching her followers into abject submission, turning them into a groveling, whining, and squirming pack of wizards and brutes. As Glaucus approached,

>            Groanings swell'd,
> Poisonous about my ears, and louder grew,
> The nearer I approach'd a flame's gaunt blue,
> That glar'd before me through a thorny brake.
> This fire, like the eye of the gordian snake,
> Bewitch'd me towards; and I soon was near
> A sight too fearful for the feel of fear:
> In thicket hid I curs'd the haggard scene—
> The banquet of my arms, my arbour queen,
> Seated upon an uptorn forest root;
> And all around her shapes, wizard and brute,
> Laughing, and wailing, groveling, serpenting,
> Showing tooth, tusk, and venom-bag, and sting![19]

The whole scene is a graphic and disturbing drama of evil and its destructive power. The laughter is hysterical and demoniacal, the wailing and groaning arise from suffering and agony such as poison induces, groveling suggests destitution and abjectness, and the serpent-like writhing connotes sensuality. All life is at war with life, displaying its weapons—tooth, tusk, venom-bag, and stinger. The glare of a "flame's gaunt blue," "a thorny brake," the fire "like the eye of the gordian snake," "an uptorn forest root"—all conjure up an eerie atmosphere. All of nature is under the power of the supernatural. Glaucus' memory of Circe as his arbor queen whom he held in his arms and feasted upon as if at a banquet contrasts with this ghastly scene, benumbing in its fearfulness.

These images dealing with human nature as serpent-like are expressions of idealists who lament that man has created a world of pain and ugliness because he has failed to exercise his intuitive imagination and thus has lost touch with the spiritual world of which he is a part. Loss of identity with the divinity pervading all nature transforms men into predatory beasts. Man, then, has created a human world of suffering in contrast to nature's world of contentment.

## Areas and Aspects of Man's Life and Experiences

The serpent images dealing with areas and aspects of human life and experiences are varied and extensive in range. The serpent is used, for example, in depiction of the infinite, the future coiled in sleep, an avenging Fury misguiding a cannon ball, Vice as a hydra surrounded by gaping youth, a victim under the rich man's foot, and the Spirit of Good.

Blake's image in which he deplores the power of thought to reduce the infinite to a finite serpent is stimulating and thought-provoking. Again, his poetry is so packed with symbolism that any attempt to analyze the imagery necessitates a consideration of its symbolic meaning. Blake frequently uses the serpent as an epithet equivalent to the material, and so contrary to the spiritual. The material world is the area of thought, or analytic reason, and the senses; the spiritual world is the sphere of the intuitive imagination. When humanity finds itself operating under rules formulated according to the dictates of reason and the senses, spiritual degeneracy begins. Blake saw Europe in this condition at the end of the eighteenth century. The following image epitomizes the power of the flesh and the power of thought, or analytic reason, to distort man's view of the infinite and his relation to it:

> Thought chang'd the infinite to a serpent, that
> which pitieth
> To a devouring flame; and man fled from its face
> and hid
> In forests of night: then all the eternal forests
> were divided
> Into earths rolling in circles of space, that like
> an ocean rush'd
> And overwhelmed all except this finite wall of flesh.
> Then was the serpent temple form'd, image of infinite
> Shut up in finite revolutions; and man became an
> Angel,
> Heaven a mighty circle turning, God a tyrant crown'd.[20]

Thought transforms the infinite and its attributes of pity and love into a serpent of lust, a devouring flame. Frightened, man flees and hides behind a veil of mortal errors,[21] "forests of night." Hidden behind his physical frailties, man no longer sees the "eternal forests"—the spiritual universe—as a unity but only as separate and unrelated pieces. Oneness has become a plurality of circles floating in space. Only when man's vision becomes blinded to the wholeness of the universe does he grow conscious of space, which like an ocean engulfs everything except the body, the finite wall of flesh. With his immortal soul separated from the infinite, man can only simulate by building a temple such as reason and the senses can design. In this process of limiting the infinite, and having lost his own divinity, man reverses all values: He sees himself as an angel (deluded, of course), encloses Heaven within boundaries, and turns God into a ruling despot and places on his head a crown—a finite revolution. Man's reason has imposed its own limitations upon the infinite, which only the intuitive imagination can apprehend completely and perfectly.

The last of the *Ecclesiastical Sonnets,* which express Wordsworth's homage to tradition and the Established Church, is built on the image of the future as a coiled serpent sleeping at noontide:

> Why sleeps the future, as a snake enrolled,
> Coil within coil, at noontide? For the Word
> Yields, if with unpresumptuous faith explored,
> Power at whose touch the sluggard shall unfold
> His drowsy rings.[22]

Even though the snake lies coiled in sleep and sluggishness at the peak of the day, the slightest stimulation stirs him out of his drowsy folds into purposeful and meaningful action. Latent power becomes visible and demonstrated power. The future, too, lies coiled, quiet, and impenetrable but, like the serpent, can be stirred into meaning and responsiveness. The power which can stir the future and render it meaningful is that yielded by the Bible when explored with care and an unpresuming faith. The light shed by the Bible as to the past, present, and future and their meaning is just as adequate as that which the sun at midday provides. If the snake and the future lie inert and seemingly unfathomable, the slightest touch or the power yielded by a faithful reading of the Bible will stir each into responsiveness. Just as disturbing the sleeping snake causes him to release the latent power in his coils, so can applying faith to the Word of God unfold many insights into the future.

Coleridge's imagination endows the avenging Furies with great ingenuity in dealing out punishment. Torn between love and loyalty toward his father on the one hand and the emperor on the other, Max Piccolomini weighs the results of any action which might hurt his father. A cannon ball shot into Octavio's camp will be parricidal, Max fears, for the snaky-haired Furies, adept at punishment, will seize the ball and maliciously direct it toward his father. Cautious and deliberate, the troubled son hesitates to put a weapon into the hands of the Furies:

> For when the ball
> Has left its cannon, and is on its flight,
> It is no longer a dead instrument!
> It lives, a spirit passes into it,
> The avenging furies seize possession of it,
> And with sure malice guide it the worst way.[23]

The poet's imagination which endows the Furies with ingenuity enough to conceal themselves inside the cannon ball and misdirect it creates an exciting picture, but prompts the reader to create an even more exciting one which depicts a Fury mounted astride the ball, with heels spurring its sides and head thrust forward, bearing and pulling through the wind a scourge of writhing snakes inciting both rider and the ridden to frenzied flight. The imagination twice becomes, to use the poet's words, "the shaping spirit": It shapes into meaningfulness the well of chaotic ideas within the poet and then becomes the rudder or "shaping spirit" of the reader's own imagination. Thus, imagination stirred by imagination becomes riotous.

Even though Byron's image comparing an aspect of life with a serpent is built around the conventional and mythological hydra, he conceives of this horrible monster-serpent as irresistible and most eager to please its audience. This is, indeed, a novel and effective presentation of the hydra, whom poets have berated and denounced for centuries. The hydra has been used so frequently to describe evil that one suggests the other. So when Byron, even though using the hydra to describe Vice, makes it attractive and desirable, he stops being conventional and becomes original and provocative. The hydra is the mythological serpent with nine heads, any one of which if cut off results in the appearance of two others. This characteristic of reproducing and multiplying itself so prolifically and rapidly is a favorite among poets in their description of any multifarious evil, or an evil having many sources, not to be overcome by a single effort. Note the transformation which the hydra has undergone in the hands of Byron:

> Ah, Vice, how soft are thy voluptuous ways!
> While boyish blood is mantling, who can 'scape
> The fascination of thy magic gaze?
> A Cherub-hydra round us dost thou gape,
> And mould to every taste thy dear delusive shape.[24]

Conceiving of the hydra as a cherub is startling and intriguing. One hesitates to believe that the poet would be bold enough to call Vice an angel even though he has been respectful enough to call on that rank of angels below the seraphim. One is equally hesitant to conceive of Vice as an innocent child. Vice is portrayed by Byron as a sensuous and voluptuous woman, posing as an innocent, wide-eyed, and rosy-cheeked cherub in an effort to disarm and win the attention and favors of youths, whose blood races in their veins seeking excitement, novelty, and variety of experience. And like the hydra, Vice can assume many shapes in an effort to suit the taste of any appetite. The word "gape" suggests the open-mouthed innocence of a child, the hunger and greed of the hydra, and the insatiate desire of sensuality.

Shelley's poetry contains some of the most original and interesting serpent images depicting areas and aspects of human life and experience. Always concerned with the problems of tyranny and freedom, Shelley in an effective image presents Freedom as being cleverer than Tyranny. The poet frequently uses the serpent to represent evil at odds with mankind and Freedom. Therefore, when Freedom outwits Tyranny in a practical joke, the reader wishes to join Hope in her eulogy of Freedom:

> "To the rich thou art a check,
> When his foot is on the neck
> Of his victim, thou dost make
> That he treads upon a snake."[25]

A victim oppressed too far by Tyranny is compared to a snake lying dangerously underfoot. Because the rich man's greed may render him oblivious to the dangers of the ground he tramples on, Freedom reminds him to watch his step, pretending that it is a snake rather than a neck on which he treads. The poet's withholding the word "snake" until the end of the line comes as a shock to the unsuspecting reader, who begins to feel a sort of pride that he, too, is involved in the prank which Freedom plays on Tyranny.

In another unusual and provocative image Shelley presents the Spirit of Good as a serpent. The snake-eagle combat in *The Revolt of Islam* is possibly Shelley's most celebrated presentation of the serpent as good in a struggle with evil. The Woman in this poem speaks of the two powers which hold dominion over mortal beings—Evil and Good. The Woman describes these powers:

> "The darkness lingering o'er the dawn of things,
>     Was Evil's breath and life; this made him strong
> To soar aloft with overshadowing wings;
>     And the great Spirit of Good did creep among
>     The nations of mankind, and every tongue
> Cursed and blasphemed him as he passed; for none
>     Knew good from evil."[26]

Evil is depicted as an eagle soaring above the earth and casting shadows; Good is depicted as a serpent creeping over the ground. The physical contrast between the swift, unfettered, and soaring eagle and the slow, earthbound, and creeping serpent is a forceful expression of the contrast between the Spirit of Evil and the Spirit of Good.

Shelley's abundant use of the serpent in images treating of the social and spiritual aspects of man's life provides an interesting and enlightening contrast to Keats's paucity of serpent images in this area. Shelley, a humanitarian, was deeply concerned with social problems and certain spiritual concepts which he associated with serpents and their power to plague and harm man. Keats, as apostle of beauty rather than an apostle of humanitarianism, exercised his imagination in making the physical and sensuous world as delightful as possible. Keats was interested in the question of beauty, not the question of social and spiritual life. Even though Shelley generally uses the serpent in many more images than does Keats, the extreme disparity in this particular area becomes especially meaningful when superimposed upon the background of their lives.

Keats's one serpent image in a social context treats of an emperor's avowal to punish disobedience in a subject:

> "Bring Hum to me!
>
> . . . . . . . . . . . . . . .
>
> Throw in a hint, that if he should neglect
> One hour, the next shall see him in my grasp,
> And the next after that shall see him neck'd,
> Or swallow'd by my hunger-starved asp—"[27]

Angry and frustrated at not attaining his true love, and about to marry someone he does not love, Emperor Elfinan sends for Hum, the soothsayer, who he hopes will be able to provide him with a magical solution to his problem. The possibility that Hum might delay his summons to appear or might refuse his request plunges the emperor into a consideration of the most horrible way to punish the soothsayer. He decides with much satisfaction that letting his hunger-starved asp swallow Hum will be punishment commensurate to the crime.

## Natural Phenomena and Man-made Objects

Even though the Romanticists are urged on by an instinct to escape from the world of sense perception, which is a "shadow-show" presented to them by their senses and reason, they still realize that they cannot disregard the sensuous, phenomenalistic, and rational worlds. They constantly strive to live in the world of imagination; yet they know that their bodies are earthbound and that they must adapt themselves to the demands of an earthly existence. Aware of the breach between body and soul, they are forever trying to bridge this gap and to find a correspondence between natural and man-made worlds on one hand, and the spiritual world on the other; between actuality and desire; and between reality and ideality. This is true of Wordsworth, Coleridge, Byron, Shelley, and Keats. In spite of the limitations of the shadow-world of physical entities, these poets are still attracted to its manifestations, which they use in their progress toward the spiritual realm. In other words, natural and man-made elements, objects, and phenomena can be signposts to the spiritual world, provided careful observation is supported by the intuitive imagination, a combination which is man's secret power, enabling him to apprehend the divine force energizing all life.

But Blake, the harbinger of romanticism, must not be presented as having even a limited respect for nature. His distrust of the natural world is unqualified. Nature, as he sees it, is the Devil and is the author of many evils. The other Romantic poets compare specific natural phenomena and man-made objects with

a serpent; Blake, however, indulges in no such activity but cate-
gorically denounces all of nature as a serpent. Describing Christ's
activities, Blake explains:

> His voice was heard from Zion's hill,
> And in his hand the Scourge shone bright;
> He scourg'd the Merchant Canaanite
> From out the Temple of his Mind,
> And in his Body tight does bind
> Satan & all his Hellish Crew;
> And thus with wrath he did subdue
> The Serpent bulk of Nature's dross,
> Till He had nail'd it to the Cross.[28]

Angry that man did not keep physical and spiritual impulses and
activities apart and in their proper spheres, Christ took scourge
in hand. The Mind is a spiritual temple and should be kept in-
violate; the Body is an arena for the exercise of physical impulses
and activities. Devoted to spiritual growth, the Mind must resist
any invasion by the physical and must keep up a constant guard
against permitting physical perceptions to color spiritual intui-
tions. Christ realized that the natural world as built up by the
senses and the rational faculty is subordinate and at cross-pur-
poses to the nature of the soul and its destiny. In order to dem-
onstrate this fact, Christ died on the cross. He proved to man
that spiritual nature and its needs and physical nature and its
needs are at odds. Until Christ died on the cross, man's only
inheritance was that of the flesh, capable only of sense knowledge
and experience in the phenomenalistic world. By permitting His
body to be nailed to the cross, He subdued all errors, weaknesses,
and evils which man had inherited since Eve's transgression.
Until Christ died, man had no spiritual inheritance but only an
inheritance of the flesh. All the misconceptions, deceptions, illusions, and evils resulting from man's reliance upon his sensuous
and physical impulses and activities are "Nature's dross"; all
the corrupt and false knowledge accrued by the reasoning faculty
is "Nature's dross." The senses and reason can dredge up only
dross, waste matter, refuse; the spiritual and intuitive imagination, on the other hand, rejects the dross and accepts only the

true substance. Because Blake holds that the natural world presents a deceiving and incomplete picture to man, nature is compared to a serpent, which is untrustworthy. In conversation with Crabb Robinson, he denied that the natural world is anything: " 'It is all nothing, and Satan's empire is an empire of nothing.' "[29] And in the same conversation, he said, " 'I fear Wordsworth loves Nature, and Nature is the work of the Devil. The Devil is in us as far as we are Nature.' "[30]

Blake's comments provide a timely introduction to Wordsworth, whose poetry is a reverent expression of the beauty of external nature and its power to ennoble him. Wordsworth would agree with Blake's accusation that he did love nature but would be compelled to part company with him at the end of the first independent clause. The following image exemplifies Wordsworth's capacity for seeing happiness in nature. The swans in their purity are no more sinless than were the snakes in Eden before the fall of Eve. Their happiness, too, in the triumph of love between Sir Galahad and an Egyptian maid is comparable to that of the snake before it sinned by tempting Eve into rebellion and disobedience:

> And lo! those Birds, far-famed through Love's
>     dominions,
> The Swans, in triumph clap their wings;
> And their necks play, involved in rings,
> Like sinless snakes in Eden's happy land.[31]

The fame of the swan in the dominion of love began with the sacredness to Apollo and Venus, god and goddess of grace and love, and in its representation of faultlessness and excellence is associated with the unblemished character of Sir Galahad and the Egyptian maid. When the noble knight and the innocent, chaste maid find each other, love and happiness prevail. The ring movement of the swans' long necks expresses the completeness, perfection, and harmony growing out of love such as prevailed in the Garden of Eden, where every form and aspect of life was a manifestation of God. Wordsworth epitomizes this love by representing the serpent, the most sinful of animals, as sinless. What greater expression of happiness, love, and innocence can there be than the representation of the snake as guiltless? Such is the joy of the swans when love in its purest expression triumphs in the lives of Sir Galahad and the Egyptian maid.

Coleridge's poetry yields only one image in which the serpent is used to describe natural phenomena. The image occurs in a fragment in which the poet marvels that the moon, even though traveling a fixed and circumscribed path, suffuses its light over all of nature, including a "snake-like stream" (*Fragments, No. 6,* II, 997). This is a prosaic serpent image. Many poets and poetasters at one time or another have compared a stream to a serpent.

Byron's comparison of the quiet surface of an oval lake with a coiled, sleeping serpent has much visual appeal. The village lake lies "navelled" in a wooded valley and is thus begrudgingly spared the violence of the wind, which in its fury uproots trees and lashes water. Treasuring its serenity, the lake nurtures a hatred for the wind:

> And, calm as cherish'd hate, its surface wears
> A deep cold settled aspect nought can shake,
> All coil'd into itself and round, as sleeps the snake.[32]

The oxymoron "cherish'd hate" points up the incongruity between the appearance of the quiet lake and the sleeping serpent, on one hand, and their real nature, on the other. Both appear calm and undisturbed; yet the calmness is not due to a gentle or passive nature. Beneath the cold, settled aspect of the glassy surface of the lake lie formidable strength and anger like that of a coiled, sleeping snake, which defies disturbance.

A particularly powerful and sensuous image illustrates Shelley's use of the serpent to describe natural phenomena and man-made objects. As has been noted before, a serpent in combat with a predatory bird is a common image in Shelley's poetry. The following image compares the prows of boats dashed about on a violent sea to necks of serpents in the grasp of a vulture:

> Higher and higher still
> Their fierce necks writhed beneath the tempest's scourge
> Like serpents struggling in a vulture's grasp.[33]

The image is effective in its combining visual, auditory, tactile, and kinesthetic appeal. The picture presents a vivid and terrifying struggle between will to survive and will to destroy. The tempest-scourged ocean relentlessly assaulting the boats in a desperate effort to submerge them is like a predatory vulture mercilessly clutching the serpents. The straining and fragmenting of wood and the tearing and rending of flesh, the lashing of wind and waves against the boats and the flapping wings and striking beak of the vulture, the rushing of wind and the hissing of fearful and angry snakes—all strike the ear with much force. The straining prows of the boats and the pulling, writhing necks of the serpents, the splintered wood and the ripped flesh stir the kinesthetic and tactile senses. Not only the theme of Shelley's image but the words "fierce," "writhed," "scourge," "struggling," and "grasp" lend to the general effect of power and dramatic intensity.

Keats uses the serpent in only two images describing natural phenomena and man-made objects, both of which are based on the mythological Gorgon, Medusa. Although occurring in a stanza rejected by Keats, one of these images is particularly effective in creating a scene and atmosphere of grotesqueness and horror. The poet imaginatively constructs a phantom boat such as he thinks one looking for a likely abode of melancholy would build. The rudder of this boat is a dragon's tail and its ropes are snakes pulled from Medusa's head:

> Though you should build a bark of dead men's bones
>     And rear a phantom gibbet for a mast,
> Stitch shrouds together for a sail, with groans
>     To fill it out, blood-stained and aghast;
> Although your rudder be a dragon's tail
>     Long sever'd, yet still hard with agony,
>         Your cordage large uprootings from the skull
>     Of bald Medusa, certes you would fail
>         To find the Melancholy—....[34]

Such a setting may seem a likely place to find Melancholy but, as the poet so beautifully explains in *Ode on Melancholy*, if one would seek out the haunts of Melancholy, then he should never leave the realms of joy and happiness. The whole poem is an eloquent expression of the paradoxical nature of the Romantic poets, who hold that beauty and ugliness, pleasure and pain, and happiness and sorrow are closely allied: man's capacity for one is associated with his capacity for the other.

## Pictorial Detail

Many times the serpent is presented as mere animal, interesting in its own right. The snake's color, sound, and movement are invaluable when the poets wish to enliven pictorial detail. At other times, the serpent is simply listed in a cataloguing of the forms of nature.

For example, Blake lists the serpent as one of the obstacles which Urizen had to contend with in his creation of the world of time and space:

> For he strove in battles dire,
> In unseen conflictions with shapes
> Bred from his forsaken wilderness
> Of beast, bird, fish, serpent & element,
> Combustion, blast, vapour and cloud.[35]

Wordsworth uses the serpent as mere animal enlivening pictorial detail. In the following image, the poet depicts a beautiful snake entwining itself about the neck of the statue of a child, sitting amid a thick, tangled wilderness:

> And the green, gilded snake, without
> troubling the calm
> Of the beautiful countenance, twine
> round his neck.[36]

The appearance of the "green, gilded snake" is one of many details which Wordsworth uses to create a picture of quiet and peaceful nature, removed from the strife and tumult of humanity and war.

Coleridge's presentation of the serpent as a mere animal is an unusually realistic one. Generally the snake is treated as an unfriendly animal from which man runs or at least one which he views with some apprehensiveness. So it is refreshing when Coleridge depicts the snake as scared and running from man. The poet describes the impassioned lover as he forces his way through the forest, seeking rest for his weary heart and at the same time disturbing nature. While he is winding in and out among the tangled undergrowth and climbing and descending hills,

> oft unseen,
> Hurrying along the drifted forest-leaves
> The scared snake rustles.[37]

Coleridge's *The Rime of the Ancient Mariner* provides his most excellent presentation of pictorial detail. The water snake scene (discussed as pantheism) is alive with vivid color and exciting movement.

Byron's image in which the serpent is just another animal and nothing more is based on the Biblical interpretation of the snake in the Garden of Eden. Lucifer's answers to Cain's curiosity concerning his mother's tempter in the Garden are eloquent and persuasive testimony to the snake's status as mere animal and nothing more:

> The snake *was* the snake—
> No more; and yet not less than those he tempted,
> In nature being earth also—*more* in wisdom,
> Since he could overcome them, and foreknew
> The knowledge fatal to their narrow joys.[38]

Byron states in the preface to the play that he is interpreting the serpent in its purely Biblical conception. He reminds the reader that no mention is made in Genesis that the serpent was a demon but only that it was wiser than all the other beasts: "NOW the serpent was more subtil than any beast of the field which the Lord God made."[39] Therefore, Byron and Lucifer capitalize upon this presentation of the serpent as a mere animal which, though not embodying a spirit or demon, possessed wisdom and power to persuade man. Lucifer, making a good case for himself and hoping to win Cain's confidence, asserts vehemently and with much finality that the serpent in the Garden of Eden was a mere snake, nothing more. And when

Cain persists in his questions implying the possibility of Lucifer's being the demon or spirit which assumed the form of the serpent, Lucifer scorns and rejects the idea that, even though he were capable of such a transformation, he would stoop to assume the shape of anything which dies. However categorical and supercilious in his denial of assuming the shape of a serpent and beguiling Eve, Lucifer continues to be plied with questions from Cain, who is torn by doubts and conflicts in regard to his father and mother's experience in the Garden of Eden. Growing impatient and belligerent, Lucifer adamantly accuses man of shifting blame for his failings and acquits himself of any such subversive activities. However, lest Lucifer appear derogatory and unfair to the serpent, he hastens to assure Cain that even though the snake was a mere animal not possessing a demon, it had the exceptional power to wake

> one
> In those he spake to with his forky tongue.
> I tell thee the serpent was no more
> Than a mere serpent.[40]

"It does not take a demon to beguile man," Lucifer seems to be saying to Cain and the Christian theologians. "A mere serpent is adequate to assist man in his own self-deception."

Shelley found the serpent interesting as pictorial detail. Wherever he paints a detailed picture of the phenomenalistic world, and this is often, he almost invariably includes the serpent. Scene after scene is a cataloguing of the animal and plant life inhabiting the world, oftentimes characterized by grotesqueness, decay, ruin, and devastation—an effect intensified by the presence of the serpent. In the following image, a Gothic atmosphere prevails in a panoramic view of a wasted world, where

> serpents, bony chains, twisted around
> The iron crags, or within heaps of dust
> To which the torturous strength of their last pangs
> Had crushed the iron crags.[41]

The visual impact is powerful. The scene is one of spent strength, destruction, and desolation. The unusual effect may be described

as strength overcome, movement immobilized, activity inacti-
vated. Depicting the serpent spines as chains suggests iron; death
as the great leveler has equated the serpents and the iron crags.
The unconquerable has been conquered, the indestructible
destroyed.

Intent on re-creating the phenomenalistic world to delight
man's sensuous nature, Keats at times dazzles the eye with a
rainbow of color, strikes the ear with a splash of sound, and
goads the tactile and kinesthetic senses into response. The poet
stresses the sensuous appeal of the serpent, which he often uses
to add to profuseness of detail, giving color, sound, and movement to his poetry. The famous description of Lamia in her
serpent form is a breathtaking and gorgeous mass of color and
intricate design. Hermes hears a mournful voice and, gliding
softly among the trees and bushes, comes upon

>          a palpitating snake,
> Bright, and cirque-couchant in a dusty brake.
>     She was a gordian shape of dazzling hue,
> Vermilion-spotted, golden, green, and blue;
> Striped like a zebra, freckled like a pard,
> Eyed like a peacock, and all crimson barr'd;
> And full of silver moons, that, as she breathed,
> Dissolv'd, or brighter shone, or interwreathed
> Their lustres with the gloomier tapestries—
> So rainbow-sided, touch'd with miseries,
> She seem'd, at once, some penanced lady elf,
> Some demon's mistress, or the demon's self.
> Upon her crest she wore a wannish fire
> Sprinkled with stars, like Ariadne's tiar:
> Her head was a serpent, but ah, bitter-sweet!
> She had a woman's mouth with all its pearls complete:
> And for her eyes: what could such eyes do there
> But weep, and weep, that they were born so fair?
> As Proserpine still weeps for her Sicilian air.
> Her throat was serpent, but the words she spake
> Came, as through bubbling honey, for Love's sake.[42]

Although the other Romantic poets depict some beautiful snakes,
they are not a threat to Keats's supremacy in this area. Blake's

serpent is frequently attired in rich and dazzling gems and adorned with a crest of fire, and Coleridge's water snakes in *The Rime of the Ancient Mariner* are colorful and scintillating. But these or other serpents cannot compare to Keats's serpent, possessing a beauty which heightens and sustains the reader's excitement for twenty-one lines. Serpent imagery in *Lamia* is organic; there would not be a poem without it.

# IV

## Serpent Symbolism in the Major Romantics

By ITS VERY NATURE, symbolism can hardly be classified into rigid and well-defined categories, but some logical demarcation is possible. Serpent symbolism in the poetry of the six major Romanticists is classified into five categories: the serpent as symbol of "Idealism," "The Fall of Man," "Materialism," "Man Against Man," and "Institutions Against Man." The categories include representative images and proceed from the positive aspects of the serpent as symbol to its most negative aspects. The reader, then, is permitted to see the Romanticists' view of a world deteriorating from a perfect, idealistic condition of love, innocence, and harmony to an imperfect, materialistic condition of hatred, guilt, and discord. The use of the serpent to symbolize the best kind of world and its various aspects, and then its use to symbolize the worst kind of world, testify to the great symbolic value of the serpent. As was noted earlier in the first chapter, no literary movement has lent itself to a greater expression of symbolism than Romanticism, and no animal has lent itself to more symbolical interpretation than the serpent.

### Idealism

#### Imagination

Idealism stresses the spirit; materialism stresses the body. Imagination, particularly the intuitive imagination, is the faculty which enables one to transcend the physical world and apprehend

74

the spiritual world. Analytic reason and the senses deal with the visible; imagination deals with the invisible. Reason and the senses capture the discord in the world; imagination captures the musical perfection. Deprecating the chaos, disorder, and fragmentation of the eighteenth-century world of reason, the Romanticists found their imagination in rebellion against the limits of reality. Blake's poetry is permeated with the theme of man's separation from the Divine. The extent to which man is imaginative determines the extent to which he is divine. "Imagination is the Divine Body in Every Man."[1] And again, speaking of the poet, Blake says, "One Power alone makes a poet: Imagination, The Divine Vision."[2] The Romantic poets held that appearances are not always what they seem, and it is only by exercise of the imagination that man can strip away illusions and get to the core of life.

So when the Romantic poets use the serpent to symbolize some aspect of idealism, they may be saying that appearances are deceiving and that frequently behind the mask of ugliness lie truth, beauty, and goodness. What appears harmful to the reasoning man may be beneficial to the imaginative man. The Romanticists' use of the serpent to symbolize imagination, benevolence, and pantheism is a superlative expression of the disparity between appearance and reality.

Keats's *Lamia* is an excellent example of not only the serpent as symbol of imagination but also of the difference in the views of reasoning and imaginative men. To Apollonius, the old man of philosophy, Lamia is evil and corruptive; but to Lycius, the young man of poetry, perhaps Keats himself, the serpent-woman is imagination, a constructive force. Claude Lee Finney, interpreting Lamia as the representation of the poetic imagination, writes:

> Keats believed that the chief function of the imagination is to understand and to represent the instincts, the passions, and the thoughts of human beings. Lamia has this imaginative insight into human nature and she has in particular intuitive knowledge of love.[3]

She is an enchantress bringing great beauty, magic, and happiness—in other words, poetry—into Lycius' life until she is stripped of all illusions by the cold, unimaginative eye of Apollonius, who exposes her despite her protest to him to be silent:

> No!
>
> "A serpent!" echoed he; no sooner said,
> Than with a frightful scream she vanished:
> And Lycius' arms were empty of delight,
> As were his limbs of life, from that same night.
> On the high couch he lay!—his friends came
>  round—
> Supported him—no pulse, no breath they found,
> And, in its marriage robe, the heavy body wound.[4]

Bereft of the beautiful Lamia and the world of imagination, Lycius dies.

Coleridge's poem *The Rime of the Ancient Mariner* provides another interesting study of the serpent in relation to the imaginative world.[5] Although the water snakes may not directly symbolize imagination, they symbolize the beauty and truth of a world which the creative imagination has wrought. The mariner's imagination transubstantiates the water snakes from the category of the loathsome and accursed to the category of the blessed and beautiful:

> Beyond the shadow of the ship,
> I watched the water-snakes:
> They moved in tracks of shining white;
> And when they reared, the elfish light
> Fell off in hoary flakes.
>
> Within the shadow of the ship
> I watched their rich attire:
> Blue, glossy green, and velvet black,
> They coiled and swam; and every track
> Was a flash of golden fire.
>
> O happy living things! no tongue
> Their beauty might declare:
> A spring of love gushed from my heart,
> And I blessed them unaware:
> Sure my kind saint took pity on me,
> And I blessed them unaware.[6]

Lowes praises *The Rime of the Ancient Mariner* as a work of pure imagination. Tracing the water snakes back to their literary birth, Lowes concludes that their appearance in Coleridge's poem is far superior to their original treatment. And this improvement is the work of the poet's imagination, a faculty which is always at work seeking beauty. The power of the imagination to transform is so great that the most repulsive phenomena become attractive. Furthermore, the uglier the phenomena the greater the power of the imagination. Lowes suspects that this "is one of the most momentous functions of the imagination—its sublimation of brute fact."[7]

N. P. Stallknecht, another Coleridge scholar, does not completely agree with Lowes that *The Rime of the Ancient Mariner* is a work of pure imagination. This critic interprets the poem not only as a work of the imagination but also as containing a moral: Man's capacity for spiritual alliance with God is determined by his capacity to love all of God's creatures. Stallknecht, however, does not wish to minimize the symbolism of the watersnake scene. The blessing of the beauty of the water snakes signifies more than just a release from suffering in atonement for the sin of killing the albatross; it symbolizes

> the importance of imagination or the faculty of esthetic enjoyment. This faculty seems to be of greatest value eudaemonistically when it apprehends the forms of Nature as beautiful. Then there may arise in the soul a profound love of man and a sense of communion with Nature or with the spirit that enlivens Nature. Thus the habitual use and the development of this faculty amplifies and strengthens the human spirit, raising it also to a life of moral freedom and happiness.[8]

Robert Penn Warren agrees with Stallknecht that *The Rime of the Ancient Mariner* combines the themes of "One Life" and imagination. He writes:

> The fusion of the theme of the "One Life" and the theme of imagination is the expression in the poem of Coleridge's general belief concerning the relation of truth and poetry, or morality and beauty.[9]

Man's imagination, then, enables him to envision the infinite and celestial in something as finite and terrestrial as the serpent.

## Benevolence

The discussion of the serpent as a symbol of benevolence includes images dealing with wisdom, sinlessness, goodness, faith, rejuvenation, eternity, and divine love. The serpent as a symbol of wisdom has a long history. Sir James G. Frazer[10] gives many accounts of ancient legends which deal with the extraordinary wisdom of the serpent. In some countries, eating the flesh of a serpent was believed to bestow supernatural wisdom upon the eater.

Then there is the Biblical association of the serpent and wisdom. Calling his twelve disciples together to instruct them regarding their behavior while on their mission among the harassed multitudes, Jesus advised: "BEHOLD, I send you out as sheep in the midst of wolves; so be wise as serpents and innocent as doves."[11]

Shelley, no doubt, recalled Jesus' words when he describes Cythna as walking quietly about the city, arming herself against scorn, death, and pain by "blending, in the smiles of that defence,/The Serpent and the Dove, Wisdom and Innocence."[12]

Shelley's equation of serpent and wisdom is not difficult to accept because the Biblical phrase "wise as a serpent" is a proverb on the lips of every advice-giver at one time or another. But when Wordsworth presents the snake as innocent and sinless, the reader is jolted into a re-examination of his thoughts about the serpent. Wordsworth says that the ring movements of swans, in a moment of happiness over love's triumph, are "Like sinless snakes in Eden's happy land."[13]

Snakes, then, contrary to the popular conception, can be considered sinless or good. Miriam J. Benkovitz tells of *Queen Mary's Psalter*, miniatures and drawings by an English artist of the fourteenth century. The Psalter pictures the serpent as a benefactor. The story of Noah's ark is presented in four plates, the last of which exhibits the return of the dove with a branch to show that land has been found. At the sight of the dove with the branch, Noah utters a cry of blessing and the devil, who is a stowaway, falls through a hole which he has made in the ark. The serpent then sticks his tail in the hole and keeps the ark afloat.

The serpent, because of his part in the seduction of Eve in the Garden of Eden, is usually considered hostile to God and to God's commands. The illustration in QMP [Queen Mary's Psalter], however, shows the serpent helping to carry out God's plan to save the world by means of the ark.[14]

At times, the serpent appears evil but is in reality good. In Shelley's *The Revolt of Islam*, the snake is presented as the Spirit of Good making its way over the earth and being abused because mankind does not always discern what is good and what is bad. The Woman in *The Revolt of Islam* speaks of the two powers which hold dominion over mortal things—Evil and Good, which are always in conflict. Evil, however, triumphed when Cain killed Abel. Then the darkness prevailing over the world gave Evil an opportunity to grow strong, develop wings, and soar like an eagle; thus the Evil Spirit as an eagle achieved mastery over the world, its wings castings ominous shadows. The Spirit of Good, however, stayed on earth in the form of a serpent:

> And the great Spirit of Good did creep among
> The nations of mankind, and every tongue
> Cursed and blasphemed him as he passed; for none
> Knew good from evil.[15]

The representation of the Spirit of Good as a serpent becomes more meaningful when one recalls the parallel incident in the Bible when the Pharisees scorned and rejected Jesus as the prophet of Nazareth. In response to his teachings, the Pharisees refused to recognize him as the son of God and conspired to entangle him in his speech. They challenged his statements, confused the issues, and were careless to distinguish truth from error. Another parallel incident illustrating the inability of people to distinguish good from evil is the Biblical account of Jesus' rejection by the chief priests and elders of the people. Unable to recognize good when it walked among them, they spat on it, cursed it, and mocked it. Shelley's conception of the Spirit of Good as a serpent which was cursed and blasphemed as it crept among the nations is bold and indicates the strength of the poet's conviction that when man is undiscerning he violates right, justice, and truth.

The serpent as symbol of the life-giving force in terrestrial matters is treated in many mythological episodes. The caduceus, the emblematic wand of Hermes, is one of the most famous representations of the serpent as a life-giving or generative force. Hermes "was the Phallic god, and the caduceus plainly denotes this, for the male and female serpents, the sun-god and moon-goddess, are symbols of generation, whilst the supporting rod or tree represents the phallus. . . ."[16]

Keats builds two images around the caduceus, which no doubt symbolizes in these instances a life-giving force or generative power. Hermes, wishing to transform the serpent into the beautiful Lamia,

> turn'd
> To the swoon'd serpent, and with languid arm,
> Delicate, put to proof the lythe Caducean charm.[17]

The other image occurs in *Endymion,* where the youth Endymion, searching for an ideal love, encounters an Indian maid, who, homesick and lovelorn, cries out in her distress for Hermes' magical wand with which to touch the hyacinth and transform it back into the youth Hyacinthus, whom Apollo had killed accidentally and from whose spilled blood the god had caused the flower to grow. The Indian maid speaks:

> "O for Hermes' wand,
> To touch this flower into human shape!
> That woodland Hyacinthus could escape
> From his green prison, and here kneeling down
> Call me his queen, his second life's fair crown!
> Ah me, how I could love!"[18]

Associated with the snake's symbolic value as a life-giving and generative force is its habit of periodically shedding its skin. This habit together with the great age which some serpents attain suggests immortality and periodic purification. In his story of Deia-

nira and Hercules, Ovid refers to the snake's habit of shedding
its skin and renewing life: Rumors reach Deianira that Hercules
loves Isole, and to prevent losing her husband she sends to him
the tunic soaked in Nessus' blood in the hope that this will revive
his failing love for her. Putting on the cloak and kindling the
flames as part of the libation ceremony and incense offering,
Hercules catches fire but is unhurt because he is in the process
of becoming a god like his father, Jove, and at the same time
throwing off all qualities given by his mother. "He kept traces
only of his father; and as a serpent, its old age sloughed off with
its skin, revels in fresh life, and shines resplendent in its bright
new scales; . . ."[19] so did Hercules forestall death.

Keats uses the serpent as symbol of rejuvenation. Glaucus,
having lost his mortality and having been forced to live as a sea-
god for a long time, is overjoyed when he sees Endymion approach. Glaucus recognizes the youth as the one who is to help
him escape from Circe's curse. As a serpent sheds its skin and
renews life, Glaucus will throw off his old life of loneliness
and sorrow and enter into a new phase. The hoary-haired sea-
god exults over his rejuvenation:

> "O Jove! I shall be young again, be young!
> O shell-borne Neptune, I am pierc'd and stung
> With new-born life! What shall I do?
>     Where go,
> When I have cast this serpent-skin of woe?"[20]

Then the old man rhapsodizes the pleasures of his new life.

Shelley also uses the serpent as a symbol of rejuvenation.
Jubilant over Greece's regaining her liberty, the chorus compares
the renewal process of the earth to that of a snake which casts
its old skin:

> The world's great age begins anew,
>     The golden years return,
> The earth doth like a snake renew
>     Her winter weeds outworn.[21]

Associated with the serpent as a symbol of rejuvenation and a
life-giving force are the ideas of immortality and eternity. One

of the earliest symbols known to or imagined by man is the
mystic hieroglyph of the serpent swallowing its own tail:

> The serpent is herein shown as a circle, representative of
> the eternity of God and a subtle emblem of immortality.
> Even if we regard it still as a viper it can now be thought
> of as destroying itself by its own venom. Seen thus, it
> symbolises the suicide of Death.[22]

The serpent, representing death, is destroyed by its own venom.
Thus, death destroyed, immortality results. Many writers, from
St. Augustine to Emerson, for example, have used the circle as
a symbol of God: "God is a Circle, whose Circumference is no-
where and whose Centre is everywhere." Donne in his *Devotions*
wrote that "One of the most convenient Hieroglyphicks of God is
a circle." The metaphor was borrowed from the Orientals, to
whom the serpent, swallowing its tail, was a hieroglyphic of
eternity, "because in your vast mouth you hold your Tayle,/As
coupling Ages past with times to come."[23]

Shelley doubtlessly was acquainted with the image and symbol
of the snake swallowing its tail. In two instances, the poet spells
out the symbolism. Describing Ianthe's innocence and invulner-
ability to the world's distractions, Shelley praises her intuition
which apprehends truths and enables her

> The flame to seize, the veil to rend,
> Where the vast snake Eternity
> In charméd sleep doth ever lie.[24]

He also praises the mind of man which can cast over the world
the vital flame of truth. The brightness of this flame

> charmed the lids
> Of the vast snake Eternity, who kept
> The tree of good and evil.[25]

Wordsworth's use of a coiled serpent to describe the future also
suggests a recognition of the snake as a symbol of eternity.
The poet asks: "Why sleeps the future, as a snake enrolled,/Coil
within coil, at noontide?"[26] The separate rings of the coil may
be equated with the divisions of time—past, present, and future;

and the unbroken, continuous coils of the spiral of the snake may symbolize the circle of eternity.

The idealistic and imaginative man has no difficulty in relating the coil of a serpent to the circle of eternity. Recognizing all entities as manifestations of the same Divine Spirit, he sees the whole created world as an eternal and perfect circle. The intuitive man knows that Divine Love creates a harmonious, perfect, and unified world and, thus, "makes the reptile equal to the God."[27] Such equality can exist only in a truly ideal and pantheistic world.

## Pantheism

Wordsworth's love for nature almost equates his name with the term "pantheism." Disillusioned at the chaos in man's life, the early Wordsworth, like Rousseau, believed in primitive society, a natural state unspoiled by artificialities, where the promptings of elemental emotions, uncorrupted by systems of thought or by governments, would lead man directly to truth, goodness, and beauty. It was from nature that Wordsworth took most of his subjects, and in nature he found God manifested. Throughout Wordsworth's poetry there is a yearning to escape from the man-made world to the natural world, where all entities achieve integration and where innocence and love obviate any claims to superiority, privilege, and hierarchy.

Wordsworth's love for nature extends even to the reptile. A true lover of nature is not selective and discriminatory but acknowledges and praises all life as manifestations of God. The snake in a gesture of instinctive friendliness or love toward other animals or man is the touchstone of a pantheistic world. A desire for a world in which animals live in peace not only with one another but also with man usually grows out of a discontent with the sorry state of affairs to which humanity has reduced itself.

The Wanderer, Wordsworth's friend with whom he travels in *The Excursion,* is a lover of all nature and feels that all life, even the harmless reptile, has rights which man should not violate:

> Birds and beasts,
> And the mute fish that glances in the stream,
> And harmless reptile coiling in the sun,

And gorgeous insect hovering in the air,
The fowl domestic, and the household dog—
In his capacious mind, he loved them all:
Their rights acknowledging he felt for all.[28]

Such calm pleasures among animal life contrasted sadly with the
plight to which man had brought himself because of his withdrawal from nature.

Wordsworth's next image is even more symbolical of a pantheistic world in that a human being becomes an actual recipient
of the love prompted by the instinct of animals which renders
them more understanding than does man's reason. Exiled and
isolated, Philoctetes, finding reason inadequate to heal his grief
caused by other men, is comforted by animal life, which proves
to him that love still exists:

When Philoctetes in the Lemnian isle
Like a form sculptured on a monument
Lay couched; on him or his dread bow unbent
Some wild Bird oft might settle and beguile
The rigid features of a transient smile,
Disperse the tear, or to the sigh give vent,
Slackening the pains of ruthless banishment
From his loved home, and from heroic toil.
And trust that spiritual Creatures round us move,
Griefs to allay which Reason cannot heal;
Yea, veriest reptiles have sufficed to prove
To fettered wretchedness, that no Bastile
Is deep enough to exclude the light of love,
Though man for brother man has ceased to feel.[29]

Man's inhuman treatment paralyzed Philoctetes into a cold, hard,
and unfeeling form. Yet, even though appearing rigid and un-
kind, he was not frightening even to the wildest bird, who unlike
man had the power to evoke a smile, a tear, or sigh. The bird,
acting on instinct, stirred the grief-stricken Philoctetes into expression; man, on the other hand, had transformed him into a
piece of stone. Even though fettered, man must take consolation
in the example set by animals. The most convincing testimony
that love still prevails in spite of man's hatred and injustice is

the serpent's friendliness. The instinct of animals renders them more spiritual than does the reason of man. Reason and hatred imprison man; instinct and love free him.

Coleridge generally presents the serpent in an evil or at least in a not too positive light. One of the few exceptions is the brilliant description of the water snakes, whose beauty provokes the ancient mariner into blessing them:

> Beyond the shadow of the ship,
> I watched the water-snakes:
> They moved in tracks of shining white;
> And when they reared, the elfish light
> Fell off in hoary flakes.
>
> Within the shadow of the ship
> I watched their rich attire:
> Blue, glossy green, and velvet black,
> They coiled and swam; and every track
> Was a flash of golden fire.
>
> O happy living things! no tongue
> Their beauty might declare:
> A spring of love gushed from my heart,
> And I blessed them unaware:
> Sure my kind saint took pity on me,
> And I blessed them unaware.[30]

Observe the structure of the first two stanzas: the first presents the water snakes lying beyond the shadow of the ship and the second within its shadow. Beyond the shadow and under the moonlight, the snakes lack identity: they move and rear, leave shining tracks of white, and reflect light, which appears to fall off in hoary flakes. Within the shadow of the ship, the water snakes take on life and color. Instead of moving and rearing, they now coil and swim. They are no longer colorless snakes casting off hoary flakes but are richly attired in bold, contrasting colors: blue, green, and black. The colorless white has turned vivid blue and green, and its coolness has become a warm, soft velvet black. The glistening white path is now a flash of golden fire. The cool, pale, and strange world becomes the warm,

colorful, and familiar world. Beyond the shadow is the preter-
natural world; within the shadow is the natural world. Feeling
a sense of communion with the water snakes, the mariner blesses
them and, thus, relates them to himself. The whole experience
is a revelation of a new world, in other words, a pantheistic world.

Stallknecht, interpreting the water-snake scene as "a sense of
communion with Nature or with the spirit that enlivens Nature,"[31]
and Warren, interpreting it as the "One Life" and as part of "the
serene order of the universe,"[32] imply pantheism. E. M. W.
Tillyard, however, even more specifically interprets the episode
of the mariner's blessing the water snakes as an expression of
pantheism:

> The Mariner watches them not as a past age would have
> done as moral emblems or as servants of man, or as witnesses
> of the ingenuity of God's craftsmanship, but as creatures
> with a life of their own ... Once you give animals a life of
> their own, you can easily suggest that it is just as good a
> life as human. And once you do that, you tend to confound
> the classic divisions of existence and to make no unclosable
> chasm between inanimate and animate, between spiritual
> and nonspiritual. And with these divisions gone, it is natural
> to identify God and creation and to make him both all
> phenomena and its animating spirit, ... rather than a person
> who has created his separate world out of nothing.[33]

In a true Coleridgean tone and Romantic style, D. H. Lawrence
poetizes his own feelings after an attempt to kill a snake. The
poet experiences a feeling of conflict issuing, on the one hand,
from reason and knowledge which urged him to kill a venomous
golden snake and, on the other hand, from his instinctive adoration and love which urged him to accept another of God's
creatures. Giving in to the voices within urging him to kill the
snake, he threw a piece of log at the tail of the snake which
writhed and hastened its withdrawal from the world of sunshine
into the dark hole. Immediately, however, he regretted his action
as did the ancient mariner after he killed the albatross: "And I
thought of the albatross,/And I wished he would come back,
my snake."[34]

Shelley's images of pantheism often depict a world in which all the poet's ideals, visions, and hopes are realized. Universal Love walks among all mineral, plant, animal, and human life, resolving all differences, mediating and joining hands in one allegiance. These entities are not distinct and diverse but are emanations, affections, forms, determinations, phenomena, aspects, manifestations, and positions of the one and same being, God, or Universal Love. Thus, in this pantheistic world, love vanquishes hate, justice replaces injustice, right prevails over privilege, and harmony resolves discord. A vision of the world converted to a state of bliss where all creatures live in harmony includes companionship between child and one of the most dangerous of serpents, the basilisk, which is said to kill by casting a fatal glance or by emitting a deadly blast of breath:

> —the dewy lawn,
> Offering sweet incense to the sunrise, smiles
> To see a babe before his mother's door,
> Share with the green and golden basilisk
> That comes to lick his feet, his morning's meal.[35]

All aspects of nature express mutual admiration. The grass, wet with dew, emits a sweet fragrance in tribute to the sunrise. The dewy lawn, glistening under the sun's rays, appears all smiles in witnessing the harmony between the serpent and the baby, sharing the morning meal. The basilisk, expressing his affection, licks the baby's feet; his green and gold coloring parallels the greenness of the grass and the gold of the sun and gives further testimony to the tranquility, pleasure, and consonance of this pantheistic world.

However much the idealistic Romantic poets would have liked to believe in a world so permeated with love and innocence, they were realistic enough to observe that animals frequently are antagonists of man, who must tame and teach them to be his friends. In the following Shelley image, the serpent and other animals became Marenghi's friends but only after he had tamed them: "Nor was his state so lone as you might think./He had tamed every newt and snake and toad."[36] Shelley again recognizes man's need to tame some animals into friendship. He depicts the

Witch of Atlas and the animals in a state of mutual respect and admiration but only after the beautiful and benevolent Witch has imparadised their savage natures:

> And first the spotted cameleopard came,
>     And then the wise and fearless elephant;
> Then the sly serpent, in the golden flame
>     Of his own volumes intervolved;—all gaunt
> And sanguine beasts her gentle looks made tame.[37]

For Blake, animals not only have to become tame; they also have to humanize before he can accept them into pantheism. In his prophetic works, he considers animals as part of nature, not as part of the divine; and he damns nature with the same eloquence with which Wordsworth extolls it.

Blake often represents this nature as being a serpent or as transforming man into a serpent. His attitude toward the serpent, then, is nearly always negative. This attitude toward nature and the serpent is a denial of a pantheistic world and helps to explain the almost total lack of pantheism in his poetry. Yet, the poet does see the possibility of such a world:

> And I heard Jehovah speak
> Terrific from his Holy Place, & saw the
>     Words of the Mutual Covenants Divine
> On Chariots of gold & jewels, with Living
>     Creatures, starry & flaming
> With every Colour, Lion, Tyger, Horse,
>     Elephant, Eagle, Dove, Fly, Worm
> And the wondrous Serpent clothed in gems
>     & rich array, Humanize
> In the Forgiveness of Sins according to
>     thy Covenant, Jehovah.[38]

Whenever man begins to lose his human and, thus, divine nature, because of his infraction against the unity and harmony of the eternal world, he almost invariably is transformed into a serpent; or if his body does not change completely into a serpent, then it exudes serpents. So when Blake presents the serpent as human-

izing rather than representing man when he dehumanizes, or rep-
tilizes, the image is the epitome of Blakean pantheism, in which
forgiveness of sins is of cardinal importance. The animals, for-
saking their evil behavior and sharing in the forgiveness of sins,
take on a human quality. The serpent in his material splendor
becomes the human form in its divine glory.

## The Fall of Man
### Serpent as Beguiler

The serpent as symbol of the Fall of Man has its heritage in
the story of the Garden of Eden, where man was immortal but
lost his divinity because he permitted a subtle and crafty snake to
outreason him. Before the entrance of the subversive serpent into
the Garden, man was the embodiment of intuitive truth and all
emanating virtues. Until the serpent appeared, man had not ques-
tioned God's command that he must not eat of the tree of knowledge of good and evil. But when the serpent arrived, he provoked
man to wonder why God had commanded him not to eat of one
particular tree. After planting the seed of curiosity in man about
God's action and thus building resentment against God for imposing responsibilities but denying man advantages, the serpent
then concluded that God forbade him to eat of this particular tree
because it would give him knowledge of good and evil and thus
raise man to His own level. Eve could not withstand such cogent
reasoning. The fact that God had not explained but had only
commanded made Him suspect. The temptation to know as much
as God was beyond Eve's power to resist; she plucked an apple
from the tree of knowledge of good and evil, ate, and gave some
to Adam. The story in the Old Testament is as follows:

NOW the serpent was more subtil than any beast of the
field which the Lord God had made. And he said unto
the woman, Yea, hath God said, Ye shall not eat of every
tree of the garden?

And the woman said unto the serpent, We may eat of the
fruit of the trees of the garden:

But of the fruit of the tree which *is* in the midst of the

garden, God hath said, Ye shall not eat of it, neither shall ye touch it, lest ye die.

And the serpent said unto the woman, Ye shall not surely die:

For God doth know that in the day ye eat thereof, then your eyes shall be opened, and ye shall be as gods, knowing good and evil.

And when the woman saw that the tree was good for food, and that it was pleasant to the eyes, and a tree to be desired to make one wise, she took of the fruit thereof, and did eat, and gave also unto her husband with her; and he did eat.

(Genesis 3: 1-6.)

Attention is called to the Old Testament's presentation of the serpent as just a subtle beast. No reference or implication is made of the serpent as being more than an animal. Even though a tempter, a beguiler, he was no demon or Satan. But he was the cleverest of all the beasts which Jehovah had made, stood erect, spoke with a human voice, and accomplished his mission. Man fell! The result was punishment for man and beast:

And the Lord God said unto the serpent, Because thou hast done this, thou *art* cursed above all cattle, and above every beast of the field; upon thy belly shalt thou go, and dust shalt thou eat all the days of thy life:

And I will put enmity between thee and the woman, and between thy seed and her seed; it shall bruise thy head, and thou shalt bruise his heel.

Unto the woman he said, I will greatly multiply thy sorrow and thy conception; in sorrow thou shalt bring forth children; and thy desire *shall be* to thy husband, and he shall rule over thee.

And unto Adam he said, Because thou hast hearkened unto the voice of thy wife, and hast eaten of the tree, of which I commanded thee, saying, Thou shalt not eat of it: cursed *is* the ground for thy sake; in sorrow shalt thou eat *of* it all the days of thy life;

Thorns also and thistles shall it bring forth to thee; and thou shalt eat the herb of the field;

In the sweat of thy face shalt thou eat bread, till thou

return unto the ground; for out of it wast thou taken; for dust thou *art,* and unto dust shalt thou return.

(Genesis 3: 14-19.)

Certainly all of the Romanticists were influenced no less by Milton than by the Bible in their use of the serpent. As has already been noted, Blake's luxuriously attired serpent is undeniably patterned after Eve's tempter in *Paradise Lost.* Milton's influence on the Romanticists is again evident in their conception and presentation of the serpent as the beguiler of man, tempting him to disobey and thereby fall from divinity. Their debt to Milton for serpent image and symbol, particularly the resplendent and deceiving serpent, must be acknowledged along with that to the Bible.

Blake uses Genesis 3: 15 in his drama *The Ghost of Abel.* Abel, who has been killed by Cain, is about to be buried. Jehovah calls to a grieving Adam, who answers:

> It is vain. I will not hear thee
> Henceforth! Is this thy Promise, that the Woman's
> Seed
> Should bruise the Serpent's head? Is this the
> Serpent?[39]

In the drama *Cain,* Byron presents the serpent in its Old Testament conception: The serpent who tempted Eve was just a subtle beast. In the preface, the poet reminds the reader that no mention is made in Genesis that the serpent was a demon. Thus, Lucifer, a main character in the drama, denies that he assumed the guise of the serpent in the Garden of Eden. Byron's use of the name "Lucifer" rather than "Satan" strengthens this conception. The angel Lucifer was the "lightbringer," or the "shining one," before he rebelled against God, was banished from heaven, and became Satan. When Cain suspects that Lucifer is a deceiving spirit, the latter assures him that if deception were his motive "a serpent/Had been enough to charm ye, as before."[40] But Lucifer's reference to a serpent in his denial only increases Cain's doubts and conflicts about his mother's and father's experience in the Garden of Eden. Cain's persistence in plying

Lucifer with questions makes the latter more vehement in his denial that he was a spirit or demon embodied in the snake tempting Eve. Lucifer must defend the tempter as a mere snake, nothing more:

> The snake was the snake—
> No more; and yet not less than those he tempted,
> In nature being earth also—*more* in *wisdom*
> Since he could overcome them, and foreknew
> The knowledge fatal to their narrow joys.
> Think'st thou I'd take the shape of things
> that die?[41]

Even though the snake was made of dust and clay just as man, he was wiser in that he possessed enough knowledge to tempt man into disobedience. With all due respect to the serpent's wisdom, he was still a snake, subject to death. For Cain to insinuate that the proud Lucifer would take the form of anything subject to death was an insult indeed. Lucifer denies the insinuation, but he does not wholly succeed in quieting Cain's curiosity. Persistently Cain questions. Lucifer again claims that the serpent was mere animal and though not possessing any demon did wake one

> In those he spake to with his forky tongue.
> I tell thee that the serpent was no more
> Than a mere serpent.[42]

Despite Lucifer's eloquent reasoning that he is innocent, Adah, Cain's wife (in the drama), still feels—perhaps intuits—that he is evil. Furthermore, she begins to suspect that Lucifer standing before them may simply be using their own dissatisfied and curious thoughts to tempt them to destruction. She voices her suspicions to Eve:

> But we, thy children, ignorant of Eden,
> Are girt about by demons, who assume
> The words of God and tempt us with our own
> Dissatisfied and curious thoughts—as thou
> Wert work'd on by the snake in thy most flush'd
> And heedless, harmless wantonness of bliss.[43]

However much Adah feels that Lucifer is an evil beguiler, she still cannot blame him completely. Lucifer may be a beguiler, but she suspects only as an abettor of her own self-deception. Man then, implies Byron, is his own deceiver.

The background and mythology of the Old Testament, however, saw the serpent as a demon. He was not just a subtle beast as the Old Testament states, an interpretation which was given by the original redactors around 1000 B.C. The ancient myth[44] upon which the Fall of Man was based told of two magic trees in the Garden of Eden, the tree of life and the tree of knowledge of good and evil. Man was forbidden on penalty of death to eat of either; whereas, according to the Old Testament, man was forbidden to eat only of the tree of knowledge of good and evil. The old myth states that man was forbidden to eat of both trees because God feared that man, acquiring knowledge of good and evil, might approach the throne too closely and endanger His supremacy. The serpent, a demon hostile to God, told man the way to knowledge of good and evil.

Blake's poem *To Nobodaddy* echoes this ancient myth which presents God as sitting on His throne and jealously guarding His supremacy:

> Why art thou silent & invisible,
> Father of Jealousy?
> Why dost thou hide thy self in clouds
> From every searching Eye?
> Why darkness & obscurity
> In all thy words & laws,
> That none dare eat the fruit but from
> The wily serpent's jaws?
> Or is it because Secresy gains females' loud
>     applause?[45]

The cloak of secrecy under which Nobodaddy hides his identity makes him "nobody," and his position of control makes him "daddy." Because Nobodaddy is afraid that man may attain knowledge, become more like Himself, and thus endanger His supremacy, he purposely stays hidden in the heavens, cloaks his laws in vagueness, mumbles his words, and leaves man bewil-

dered and stumbling with no recourse for help except from the
"wily serpent's jaws." Jealous Nobodaddy sits quietly on His
throne, withholding aid, thus driving man to the serpent for help.
If Nobodaddy's secrecy is not motivated by jealousy, the poet
puzzles, then perhaps it is an appeal to win the approval of all
Eves, who are also lovers of secrecy and intrigue.

The parallelism of the jealous God and the jealous Nobodaddy
appears to be interpretatively sound. Blake's wily serpent, however, differs from the ancient myth predating the Old Testament.
For Blake, the serpent symbolizes an antagonistic force—a demon,
perhaps Satan, the physical world, or spiritual degeneracy—
whereas the demon serpent of the myth was a benefactor, in
intention at least, of the human race in that he enlightened
man on how to achieve knowledge of good and evil and thus
become more like God. The only verse in the Old Testament
which retains part of the ancient myth of the Garden of Eden
is Genesis 3: 22:

> AND the Lord God said, Behold, the man is become as
> one of us, to know good and evil: and now, lest he put
> forth his hand, and take also of the tree of life, and eat,
> and live for ever:

Blake's *To Nobodaddy* could be related directly to the ancient
myth of the Fall of Man or indirectly through the fragment in
the Old Testament (Genesis 3: 22). In *Cain,* Byron also appears
to use one source or the other. Adam is frightened at Cain's
rebellious and defiant attitude when his older son questions him
as to why he did not eat of the tree of life rather than the tree
of knowledge and, consequently, defy God by securing life and
cheating death. Adam cautions Cain: "Oh, my son,/Blaspheme
not: these are serpent's words."[46]

A look at the serpent just as a subtle beast as represented in
the Old Testament and then at the ancient myth presenting the
serpent, not as Satan, but as a demon hostile to God brings us
to the New Testament, which does call the serpent "Satan" and
claims an identity of the two in the Garden of Eden. Paul makes
use of Genesis 3: 15 in his letter to the Romans in which he implies an identity between Satan and the serpent:

For your obedience is come abroad unto all *men.* I am glad therefore on your behalf: but yet I would have you wise unto that which is good, and simple concerning evil.

And the God of peace shall bruise Satan under your feet shortly.

(Romans 16: 19-20.)

Another passage in the New Testament identifies the deceiving serpent and Satan as the same entity:

And the great dragon was cast out, that old serpent, called the Devil, and Satan, which deceiveth the whole world: he was cast out into the earth, and his angels were cast out with him.

(Revelation 12: 9.)

Interpretations of the Garden of Eden story began in ancient days, continued in the Middle Ages, and are still presented in modern times. In general, Christian theologians have identified Satan as the serpent, or as the demon in the serpent, which caused the Fall of Man.

In the following image, Blake identifies the serpent in the Garden of Eden with Satan. Albion, the Eternal Man, walks among the people calling them friends and exhorting them to reject the veil which Satan, in the guise of the serpent, put between Adam and Eve. The veil symbolizes the illusion which man knows as the physical universe; and to be separated from the source of spiritual light, because he sees the perceivable world as attractive and tempting, is to assume the glittering guise of the serpent. When man permits this veil to dim his vision and to deceive him into thinking that the physical universe is reality, then it is as if he, too, has become a serpent, slithering in sensuous delight:

> ... for the Eternal Man
> Walketh among us, calling his Brothers & his Friends,
> Forbidding us that Veil which Satan puts between
> Eve & Adam,
> By which the Princes of the Dead enslave their
> Votaries,
> Teaching them to form the Serpent of precious
> stones & gold.[47]

Even though Blake identifies the serpent in the Garden of Eden with Satan, his serpent is not limited to such a narrow symbolic interpretation. Satan was not just the "devil" to Blake, who was much more expansive in his use of symbols. The serpent connotes spiritual degeneracy, faulty reasoning, self-deception, and in general materialism. The serpent is the symbol of not only the entity Satan but also the state, or condition, Satan:

> But when Luvah in Orc became a Serpent, he descended into
> That State call'd Satan.[48]

When love in Orc became passion and degeneracy, he lost his spiritual nature and entered into materialism, or the state of Satan. The state of Satan, materialism, the world of death—all are equated with the serpent. In other words, any condition which excludes, or is contrary to, the spiritual is serpentine.

## Woman as Serpent-Beguiler

Serpent symbolism has been considered with relation to the original beguiler in the Garden of Eden, Satan. The complete story of the Fall of Man, however, requires an examination of serpent symbolism and woman as a beguiler. Woman, beginning with Eve in the Bible and Pandora of Greek mythology, has also often played the role of a beautiful and beguiling creature. In Genesis the following story is told as to the creation of woman:

> And the Lord God caused a deep sleep to fall upon Adam, and he slept: and he took one of his ribs, and closed up the flesh instead thereof;
> And the rib, which the Lord God had taken from man, made he a woman, and brought her unto the man.
> And Adam said, This *is* now bone of my bones, and flesh of my flesh: she shall be called Woman, because she was taken out of Man.
>
> (Genesis 2: 21-23.)

When Adam saw Eve, he was completely pleased that the new object which God brought to him was of his own substance; therefore, he called her "woman," for "from-man" was she taken.[49]

The cynics would correct the translators of Hebrew and insist that Adam, on being shown the new object which God presented to him, exclaimed "Woe-man." It is difficult to discredit such reasoning when one remembers the grief which Eve caused Adam.

It is not too much to assume that the Romantic poets sympathized with Adam because they felt within themselves the same vulnerability to the wily serpentine qualities of woman. No one has put it more aptly than Byron, who compares the beauty of Zuleika, the bride of Abydos, to that of Eve. From the time that Eve smiled on the dreadful but lovely serpent, woman, the beguiled, became—and continues to be—the beguiler:

> Fair as the first that fell of womankind,
>> When on that dread yet lovely serpent
>> smiling,
> Whose image then was stamp'd upon her mind—
> But once beguiled and ever more beguiling.[50]

In Byron's drama *Heaven and Earth,* Raphael recognizes Anah as a serpent-beguiler, yet even more redoubtable than the snake in that she continues to tempt heavenly hosts:

> —beautiful she is,
> The serpent's voice less subtle than her kiss.
> The snake but vanquish'd dust, but she will draw
> A second host from heaven, to break heaven's law.[51]

The original serpent tempted man to destruction just once; women, implies Byron, are more formidable because they keep tempting man.

Shelley, too, is charmed by an enticing woman. In a poem addressed to his friend Edward Williams, he says of himself: "The serpent is shut out from Paradise."[52] Having lost a child, Mary and Shelley found their relationship strained and unpleasant. Mary's grief over the death of their child turned partly into resentment against Shelley, whose extreme sensitivity found comfort in the pleasant company of Edward and Jane Williams. Originally Shelley had not been attracted to Jane, as the biographer White states.[53] The more he came to know her, however, the fonder he grew of her. When his relations with Mary continued to be strained, Jane became his new idealized love. Shelley, throughout his life, like a true Romanticist, idealized many loves. Jane epitomized the warmth, understanding, and appreciation which the sensitive Shelley so badly needed. When Mary objected to such intimacy, Shelley decreased his visits but felt that the denial of such delightful company was comparable to being barred from Paradise. Calling himself a serpent is obviously his acknowledgment of being the tempter who initiated the intimacy with Jane; but Jane, the beguiled, has become the beguiler sitting within Paradise, toward which Shelley's thoughts turn.

Describing a scene where he and Jane had walked in blissful solitude, Shelley reconstructs:

> We paused amid the pines that stood
> The giants of the waste,
> Tortured by storms to shapes as rude
> As serpents interlaced.[54]

The desolation of the waste symbolizes Shelley's hardships and frustrations; the visual image of the pines twisted by storms into interlaced serpents probably symbolized for the idealistic Shelley a spiritual embrace. Of course, other symbolic interpretations, less spiritual, are possible.

Mythological explanation of the creation of woman provides an interesting analogy to the Biblical story. Throughout the Golden Age, there were no women on earth, but Zeus, growing angry that Prometheus loved men and did so much for them, swore to be revenged on mankind:

> He made a great evil for man, a sweet and lovely thing to look upon, in the likeness of a shy maiden, and all the gods gave her gifts, silvery raiment and a broidered veil, a wonder to behold, and bright garlands of blooming flowers and a crown of gold—great beauty shone out from it. Because of what they gave her they called her *Pandora*, which means "the gift of all." When this beautiful disaster had been made, Zeus brought her out and wonder took hold of the gods

and men when they beheld her. From her, the first woman,
comes the race of women, who are an evil to men, with a
nature to do evil.[55]

Classical mythology and medieval lore are rife with supernatural creatures who combine in themselves the characteristics
of both human beings and serpents in an effort to beguile men
and fulfill their own desires. They adopt land, sea, or air as their
habitat, are part woman or part snake, have the power to turn
themselves completely from one into the other, or they may just
have viperous qualities without assuming the actual form.

In *Endymion,* Keats tells of the mythological Circe, a beautiful
enchantress, who bewitches others into unquestioning submission.
Glaucus, a sea-god, tells Endymion how Circe charmed him into
forgetting his ideal love, Scylla, until one morning when, discovering the seductress missing from his side, he went to search
for her and found her exercising her serpent wiles upon the
forest shapes. Glaucus describes Circe's evil power:

> Groanings swell'd
> Poisonous about my ears, and louder grew,
> The nearer I approach'd a flame's gaunt blue,
> That glar'd before me through a thorny brake.
> This fire, like the eye of gordian snake,
> Bewitch'd me towards; and I soon was near
> A sight too fearful for the feel of fear:
> In thicket hid I curs'd the haggard scene—
> The banquet of my arms, my arbour queen,
> Seated upon an uptorn forest root;
> And all around her shapes, wizard and brute,
> Laughing, and wailing, groveling, serpenting,
> Showing tooth, tusk, and venom-bag, and sting![56]

Watching Circe hypnotize the forest wizards and brutes, who
were once men, into groveling and "serpenting" shapes, Glaucus
then knew that he, too, was a victim of this beautiful but evil
enchantress.

Robert Burton's *The Anatomy of Melancholy* is a fertile source
of literary plots, one of which is the legend of the lamia, a serpent-woman.[57] Burton takes from Philostratus' *de vita Apolloni*

the memorable instance of a serpent assuming the guise of a beautiful young woman to charm Menippus Lycius into submission:

> ... Menippus Lycius, a young man twenty-five years of age, that going between Cenchreas and Corinth, met such a phantasm in the habit of a fair gentlewoman, which taking him by the hand carried him home to her house in the suburbs of Corinth, and told him she was a Phoenician by birth, and if he would tarry with her, "he would hear her sing and play, and drink such wine as never any drank, and no man should molest him; but she being fair and lovely would live and die with him that was fair and lovely to behold." The young man, a philosopher, otherwise staid and discreet, able to moderate his passions, though not this of love, tarried with her awhile to his great content, and at last married her, to whose wedding amongst other guests, came Apollonius, who by some probable conjectures, found her out to be a serpent, a lamia, and that all her furniture was like Tantalus's gold described by Homer, no substance, but mere illusions. When she saw herself descried, she wept, and desired Apollonius to be silent, but he would not be moved, and thereupon she, plate, house, and all that was in it, vanished in an instant: "many thousands took notice of this fact, for it was done in the midst of Greece."[58]

Burton's story is the source of Keats's famous poem *Lamia*, in which a serpent-woman enchants the youth Lycius and brings great beauty, magic, and happiness into his life until she is exposed by Apollonius, the Sophist philosopher. Her power broken, she vanishes. Bereft of his beautiful enchantress, Lycius dies. The following image portrays both the serpent and human qualities of Lamia. She was

> a palpitating snake,
> Bright, and cirque-couchant in a dusky brake.

> She was a gordian shape of dazzling hue,
> Vermilion-spotted, golden, green, and blue;
> Striped like a zebra, freckled like a pard,
> Eyed like a peacock, and all crimson barr'd;
> And full of silver moons, that, as she breathed,
> Dissolv'd or brighter shone, or interwreathed

Their lustres with the gloomier tapestries—
So rainbow-sided, touch'd with miseries,
She seem'd at once, some penanced lady elf,
Some demon's mistress, or the demon's self.
Upon her crest she wore a wannish fire
Sprinkled with stars, like Ariadne's tiar:
Her head was a serpent, but ah, bitter-sweet!
She had a woman's mouth with all its pearls complete:
And for her eyes: what could such eyes do there
But weep, and weep, that they were born so fair?
As Proserpine still weeps for her Sicilian air.
Her throat was serpent, but the words she spake
Came, as through bubbling honey, for Love's sake.[59]

Lycius could not resist such beauty. His unfortunate experience is another notable example of man's succumbing to a fascinating and beguiling woman.

## Materialism

The enmity between Romanticism and materialism can be expressed as the enmity between spirit and matter, the supernatural and nature, intuition on the one hand and reason and the senses on the other, between abstraction and concretion, imagination and reality, subjectivity and objectivity, symbol and sign, shadow and substance, the intangible and tangible, the non-arbitrary and arbitrary, the massive and focal, connotation and denotation, interpretation and expression, creativity and discovery, and faith and facts.

### Analytic Reason

The whole Romantic period is a protest against the materialism of the eighteenth century with its emphasis on analytic reason, empiricism, and sensuousness, which deal only with the physical and tangible world. Reason is a serpent dangerous and misleading to man. If not a serpent itself, then it has the power to convert nature, the infinite, and man himself into a serpent. A human being is born with intuitive power, but as he grows older, he begins to reason and to neglect his intuition. This imbalance brings the conscious into play and disregards the unconscious, an idea which Wordsworth expresses in *Intimations of Immortality*. Both Blake and Wordsworth lament the errors of the "meddling intellect," which can dissect for analysis of the parts but still cannot comprehend the nature of the unity as contained in the whole. Reason opens up the opposite and shows conflicts and contradictions but lacks the power to reconcile these contradictions.

The serpent symbolizes for Blake the inadequacy of analytic reason to apprehend spiritual truth. When man relies upon his reason to guide him, then he is permitting himself to be strangled in the constrictions of a deceiving serpent. Blake believed this misconception to be the source of the evils of Europe during the eighteenth century. With reason at work and intuition asleep, humanity relinquishes its greatest power, advancing materially but declining spiritually.

Blake deplores the state to which the serpent reasonings of Bacon, Newton, and Locke have reduced Albion, who for Blake symbolizes the Universal or Eternal Man. Deprived of spiritual vision, man relies upon reason, which is a spectre paralyzing and destructive. Blake prays:

> O Divine Spirit! sustain me on thy wings,
> That I may awake Albion from his long and cold repose!
> For Bacon & Newton, sheath'd in dismal steel, their
>     terrors hang
> Like iron scourges over Albion. Reasonings like
>     vast Serpents
> Infold around my limbs, bruising my minute articu-
>     lations.[60]

Having lost eternity because of his apostasy, Albion tosses about in his agony of broodings on the past, and in a desire for comfort and refuge draws England to his breast but is repelled because the spectre reason tyrannizes over her. She stretches out against him like a long serpent:

> Then Albion drew England into his bosom in groans
>     & tears,
> But she stretch'd out her starry Night in Spaces
>     against him like
> A long Serpent in the Abyss of the Spectre.[61]

The serpent plays a prominent part in Blake's poem *The French Revolution.* Alarmed at the devastation prevalent in Europe during the latter half of the eighteenth century while in the grip of the reasonings of Locke, Hume, Newton, and Bacon, Blake depicts man as hidden and chained in a dungeon and "In his soul was the serpent coil'd round his heart."[62]

Coleridge, too, realizes the inadequacy of reason to elevate man to dignity and divinity. Exercise of reason furnishes no light for man's penetration of the natural, material world and for entrance into the supernatural world. Reason, or analytic thought, deals with the visible; intuition deals with the invisible. Reason may recognize the material world as expression, but only intuition can go beyond expression to attain the spirit which prompts the expression. The urge back of the manifestation is more important than the manifestation to the Romanticists; conversely, expression is more important than the prompting urge to the reasoner. In an effort to dispel the gloom resulting from reason's paralyzing restrictions, Coleridge banishes his enemy: "Hence, viper thoughts, that coil around my mind,/Reality's dark dream!"[63] Only the intuitive imagination can apprehend the real beauty and truth immanent in the universe.

So damaging is the power of reason that it converts the infinite into a serpent. By using reason, man places his own limitations upon the infinite. Blake condemns the reasonings of Europe's eighteenth-century philosophers and scientists for turning the infinite into the finite:

> Thought chang'd the infinite to a serpent,
>
> . . . . . . . . . . . . . . . . . . .
>
> Then was the serpent temple form'd, image of
>      the infinite
> Shut up in finite revolutions, and man became
>      an Angel,
> Heaven a mighty circle turning, God a tyrant
>      crown'd.[64]

As has already been pointed out in Chapter III, where this serpent image is discussed under the category dealing with areas and aspects of human life and experience, man's reason is capable only of building a temple to represent his conception of God. Man's reason misleads him into elevating himself to the rank of an angel, demoting God to a crowned tyrant, and placing heaven within boundaries.

## Empiricism

Another aspect of materialism is empiricism, which attributes all knowledge to experience of the senses. Since the Romanticists stress the world of nature as a manifestation of God, the Divine Spirit, or the Absolute, only intuition can understand that which lies beyond the physical world. The Romanticist intuits the wholeness of the universe and stresses the unity of things of the world and, thus, is temperamentally unable to have patience with the empiricist, who accepts nothing as valid except that which the senses confirm. The senses present a piecemeal approach to the universe. If one wholeheartedly seeks the secret strength in the universe and recognizes himself as a miniature of this strength, then he exercises his intuition and recognizes every manifestation as the Absolute's urge to self-expression. The Romanticists stress the spirit of man and deprecate the inadequacy of sense experience to nourish that spirit. Intuition is the testing ground of truth, and the more frequently man exercises intuition the more accurately he apprehends the relationship between the divinity within himself and the larger divinity pervading the universe. Distrusting the senses as the sources of truth, the Romanticists feel sorry for the earth-bound empiricists. Yet, if the empiricists refuse to exercise intuition, they drag their souls through the mire of the material world instead of releasing them to soar with the Absolute, or the Infinite, in its illimitable, expansive flight. Left to the experience of the senses, the material world is a serpent deceiving man, or is a habitat fit only for serpents.

Blake's poetry is a violent protest against a materialistic world. He saw all of Europe at the end of the eighteenth century in the grip of a materialistic philosophy and lamented the devastation resulting from humanity's reliance on reason and the senses. The empiricists are personal enemies of Romanticism. Their insistence that the inductive method is the only acceptable method for discovering truth, that the mind at birth is a *tabula rasa* to be filled with content derived from sense experience, that there is no such thing as hypothetical deduction, and that phenomena are the only valid source of truth finds no sympathy among the intuitive Romanticists. All empiricists suspect the intuitive mind and heart as being like those uneven mirrors which impart their own properties to different objects and thus distort them. The Romanticists, on the other hand, exalt both the intuitive mind and the feeling heart in their power to apprehend universal truths. Sense experience gives only a fragmented, half-formed picture of the universe. The material world of physical entities may satisfy the senses but not man's spirit.

Blake presents a chilling picture of human beings groveling over the earth like serpents exercising only their senses and missing the Great Light visible only to those who keep their human and divine form, stand upright, and permit their intuition to lead them upward above the physical world. Satisfying the senses requires communication with the ground:

> "Ah! shut in narrow doleful form,
> Creeping in reptile flesh, upon the bosom of the ground!
> The Eye of Man, a little narrow orb clos'd up & dark,
> Scarcely beholding the Great Light, conversing with
>     the ground;
> The Ear, a little shell, in small volutions shutting
>     out
> True Harmonies, & comprehending great as very small;
> The Nostrils, bent down to the earth & clos'd with
>     senseless flesh,
> That odours cannot them expand, nor joy on them
>     exult;
> The Tongue, a little moisture fills, a little food
>     it cloys,
> A little sound it utters, & its cries are faintly
>     heard."[65]

A similar description of man controlled by the senses appears in Blake's *Milton* and is followed by a contrast between the minuscule senses and the great and grand aspects of the infinite. Because man's senses, like his reason, cannot apprehend the spiritual, they reduce the infinite to finiteness. Thus, the reasoner and the sensist place their own limitations upon the infinite. But listen to Blake's beautifully clear protest against the inadequacy of the senses to apprehend the divine pleasures:

> "Can such an Eye judge of the stars? & looking
>     thro' its tubes
> Measure the sunny rays that point their spears
>     on Udanadan?
> Can such an Ear, fill'd with the vapours of the
>     yawning pit,
> Judge of the pure melodious harp struck by a
>     hand divine?
> Can such closed Nostrils feel a joy? or tell of
>     autumn fruits
> When grapes & figs burst their covering to the
>     joyful air?
> Can such a Tongue boast of the living waters?
>     or take in
> Ought but the Vegetable Ratio & loathe the faint
>     delight?
> Can such gross Lips percieve? alas, folded within
>     themselves
> They touch not ought, but pallid turn & tremble
>     at every wind."[66]

Udanadan, a state of non-visionary life, values the vegetative rather than the spiritual and intuitive world.

Reliance on the senses transforms not only man himself into a serpent but also the whole world of nature, deluding man and leading him into a state of error and evil. Ahania, representing eternal reason as opposed to sense and reason and still devoted to Urizen in her memory of him as a perfect being, pleads with him not to set himself against the Eternal Man, Albion, who is still part of the Divine Unity. Urizen has separated himself from Eternity and created a world of sense experience. To strengthen her argument that dire consequences will follow if Urizen attempts to deceive others into thinking that the material world is adequate, Ahania relates the doom of Vala and Luvah, who urged man to embrace the sense-perceivable world as the true world. For rejection of the spiritual world and acceptance of the material world, Vala and Luvah found themselves falling into a state of death, or a non-visionary existence of pain and suffering, and as they fell, "the vast form of Nature, like a Serpent, roll'd between."[67] Again in *Jerusalem* nature is compared to a serpent.[68]

Blake's poetic protest against nature is no less formidable than his denunciation in prose: ". . . for whoever believes in Nature . . . disbelieves in God. For Nature is the work of the Devil."[69]

## Sensuousness

Sensuousness, another aspect of materialism, stresses the value of possessing wealth, satisfying bodily needs, and pursuing other pleasures of the flesh. Sensuousness together with spirituality was not criticized by the Romanticists. Only when these sensuous pleasures were unnaturally restricted by conventional morality or unnaturally expressed through conventional materialism did the Romanticists protest. Sensuousness as a serpent of materialism could not be tolerated.

In mythology the Iron Age was the symbol of materialism, the symbol of sensuousness. It was the last and worst age of the world, succeeding the Golden, Silver, and Brazen Ages. During the Iron Age, truth, modesty, honor, and virtue fled; and crime, violence, cunning, lust, and desire for material gain prevailed. The earth up to this time had been shared harmoniously but now was divided into separate plots for individual ownership. Men, not being satisfied with what the surface produced, dug into its bowels for ores of metals. "Mischievous *iron*, and more mischievous *gold*, were produced. War sprang up, using both as weapons."[70] Discord grew in the home and among relatives. All envied the other's wife or material possessions. The world was rife with toil, blame, and degeneracy.

In *Prometheus Unbound*, Shelley associates iron and serpents, a connection which may point to the sensuousness, toil, and degeneracy of the Iron Age. After the unbinding of Prometheus, who is the epitome of spiritual development, the world rejoices that good has triumphed over the evils of Jupiter and his tyrannous reign, under which the Iron Age occurred. Panthea, the spirit of intuition and faith, exults in retrospect that these evils and errors are now of a cancelled cycle. Describing Jupiter's materialistic world—characterized by toil, greed, self-perpetuation, and sensuousness—Panthea sees as part of this desolate scene

> serpents, bony chains, twisted around
> The iron crags, or within heaps of dust
> To which the tortuous strength of their last pangs
> Had crushed the iron crags.[71]

Blake, too, frequently associates iron and serpents. Comparison of Urizen's backbone to both a serpent and an iron chain suggests the degeneracy and selfishness of Urizen's non-visionary, materialistic world:

> Los beheld
> Forthwith, writhing upon the dark void,
> The Back bone of Urizen appear
> Hurtling upon the wind
> Like a serpent! like an iron chain
> Whirling about in the Deep.[72]

Again Blake associates snakes and iron, and speaks against the terrors of materialistic philosophers, which keep Albion, the Eternal Man, earth-bound:

> For Bacon & Newton, sheath'd in dismal steel,
>     their terrors hang
> Like iron scourges over Albion: Reasonings
>     like vast serpents
> Infold around my limbs, bruising my minute
>     articulations.[73]

In *Vala, or The Four Zoas,* Blake again deplores Urizen's materialistic world. Under his inflexible laws, men can exercise no moral choice and, being forced to live by their senses, they become like serpents intent on satisfying physical urges. Forced to rely on their senses and denied moral and spiritual freedom, they live close to the ground and fight for survival. Perpetuation of selfhood becomes the controlling factor. They rage, war, pursue women in a desire to beget, devour food, and place emphasis on the material splendors of the world. When Orc, the Prince of Love, succumbs to the temptations of Urizen's material world, he

becomes the embodiment of passion and rage and thereby dis-
integrates into

> . . . a Serpent wondrous among the Constellations
>     of Urizen.
> A crest of fire rose on his forehead, red as the
>     carbuncle,
> Beneath, down to his eyelids, scales of pearl,
>     then gold & silver
> Immingled with the ruby overspread his Visage down
> His furious neck; writhing contortive in dire
>     budding pains
> The scaly armour shot out. Stubborn, down his
>     back & bosom
> The Emerald, Onyx, Sapphire, jasper, beryl, amethyst
> Strove in terrific emulation which should gain a
>     place
> Upon the mighty Fiend, the fruit of the mysterious
>     tree
> Kneaded in Uveth's kneading trough. Still Orc
>     devour'd the food
> In raging hunger. Still the pestilential food,
>     in gems & gold,
> Exuded round his awful limbs, Stretching to
>     serpent length
> His human bulk, while the dark shadowy female,
>     brooding over,
> Measur'd his food morning & evening in cups &
>     baskets of iron.[74]

Blake's serpent is nearly always luxuriously attired in exquisite
gems, dancing, sparkling, and vying for the most enviable position on the serpent's body. The exquisite gems are not only serpent Orc's attire but also his food, which he devours with such
gluttony that it exudes from his body. Only a trough is capacious
enough for Orc's ravenous hunger. It is interesting to note that
the cups and baskets in which Urizen's handmaiden measures
Orc's food are made of iron, again suggestive of mythological
man's use of metals when he degenerated into a warring, lustful,
and acquisitive plunderer.

It is not surprising that the intuitive, subjective, and emotional man of the nineteenth century saw the eighteenth century as the Age of Reason or the Age of Iron or the Age of Materialism. Emphasis on the senses and their reliability to report truthfully and accurately the meaning of the physical world, man's regard for matter and disregard of the spiritual, his self-confidence that the mind could reason the truth rather than intuit it—all these aspects of the eighteenth century, as the Romanticists saw it, left man bound with the iron fetters of analytic reason, limited by the yoke of empiricism, and consumed by sensuousness and degeneracy.

## Man Against Man

### Enmity

When man falls from a spiritual to an earthly existence, embracing a materialistic world, then, according to Blake,

> he has enter'd that State,
> A world where Man is by Nature the
> enemy of Man.[75]

All the Romantic poets stress the serpent as the symbol of enmity between men, who in their desire for self-perpetuation, power, and recognition have forsaken the love of God and fellow man. Love of self dominates all thoughts and actions. When man depends upon his reason and senses and sees nothing beyond the material world, then the self seems to be the center of the world and all else an enemy if it does not feed that self's vanity.

In contrast to Blake's emphasis on materialism as the cause of enmity between men, the cynical Byron places the blame on instinct and not on some external cause. In Byron's drama *Werner, or The Inheritance*, Stralenheim, in his effort to gain for himself a fortune left to Werner, feels a natural antipathy when he comes face to face with Ulric, Werner's son:

> ... the antipathy with which we met,
> As snakes and lions shrink back from each other
> By secret instinct that both must be foes
> Deadly, without being natural prey to either.[76]

Antipathy between men is like that of snakes and lions, a hatred growing out of instinct, not experience. For Byron, experience is not needed to corrupt man; his basic nature and inheritance are corrupt enough.

The serpent images under discussion include manifestations of enmity ranging from a suppressed feeling of dislike to an act of murder. Between the extremes of this gamut lie serpent images dealing with slander, falsity, treachery, malicious hypnotic power, unreciprocated love, and hatred. These expressions of enmity occur, for example, between political figures, friends, lovers, mother and son, father and sons, brother and brother, and slaves and liberators.

Keats uses the serpent's breath to symbolize slander. He is probably referring to the basilisk, a mythological serpent which was able to kill by emitting a deadly vapor. There is a legend telling of a serpent's ability to assume the form of a human being but an inability to rid himself of the forked tongue and foul breath.[77] In *Otho the Great,* Ethelbert, knowing of Conrad and Auranthe's slander against Princess Erminia's character, acknowledges their viperous quality. Ethelbert asks himself:

> Yet why do I delay to spread abroad
> The names of those two vipers from whose jaws
> A deadly breath went forth to taint and blast
> This guileless lady?[78]

The serpent frequently symbolizes falseness. In Shelley's drama *The Cenci,* Beatrice feels that she has been unjustly condemned to die for the murder of her father, who was evil and deserved death. She is saddened by her brother's betrayal and the world's injustice. She sings a song to a false friend, presumably her brother: "There is a snake in thy smile, my dear;/And bitter poison within thy tear."[79]

Coleridge compares the charming but treacherous Octavio Piccolomini to an adder, who flatters his friend Wallenstein and thus secures freedom to do malice without incurring suspicion. Wallenstein, discovering Octavio's betrayal, denounces him:

> The adder! O, the charms of hell o'erpowered me.
> He dwelt within me, to my inmost soul
> Still to and fro he passed suspected never![80]

Byron also presents the serpent as symbol of treachery. Sardanapalus, King of Nineveh and Assyria, chides Arbaces, the Mede
who aspires to the throne, that it is his treachery and not his
strength which is dreaded:

> We dread thy treason, not
> Thy strength: the tooth is nought without
>     its venom—
> The serpent's, not the lion's.[81]

Physical strength, like that of the lion, can be opposed; treachery,
however, secretive and devious, is more formidable.

An interesting concept to poets is that of the adder's stopping
its ears to avoid being charmed. This concept has its heritage
in the Old Testament, where the wicked are described:

> Their poison *is* like the poison of a serpent: *they are* like
> the deaf adder *that* stoppeth her ear;
> Which will not hearken to the voice of charmers, charming
> never so wisely.
>
> (Psalms 58: 4-5.)

Coleridge uses this Biblical concept in an image dealing with a
woman's hypnotic power. The tortured lover feels that both he
and the woman are guilty of crimes, he for feeling too much
passion, and she for disdaining him. Bewitched by the lady's
hypnotic eye, yet scorned by her deaf ear, the lover feels himself to be under the spell of a serpent: "I fascinated by an
Adder's eye—/Deaf as an Adder thou to all my pain."[82]

Coleridge's poem *Christabel* is probably the most famous treatment of a human being's assuming serpentine qualities to hypnotize another. In this poem, Lady Geraldine casts a spell over
Christabel. Just what specific evil Geraldine wishes to do Christabel is vague, but that she is evil is generally accepted. Although
Geraldine is a beautiful lady and appears to be like other human
beings, she soon reveals specific characteristics which mark her as
inhuman and malevolent. The gems entangled in her hair may
suggest the snake frequently depicted with brilliant gems in its
head. More specific attributes of Geraldine as a serpent are the
hissing sound, the dilation and contraction of the eyes, and the

power to charm Christabel. Bard Bracy dreams that a dove is in trouble in the forest. Disturbed, he resolves to learn the cause of the dove's trouble. Stooping to pick up the bird, he sees

> a bright green snake
> Coiled around its wings and neck.
> Green as the herbs on which it couched,
> Close by the dove's its head it crouched;
> And with the dove it heaves and stirs,
> Swelling its neck as she swelled hers![83]

Bard Bracy's dream intensifies the presentation of Geraldine as evil and wishing to control. Sir Leoline, however, equating Geraldine with the dove and her offender with the serpent, promises to kill the snake. At this time, Geraldine assumes the position of the snake in Bard Bracy's dream:

> And folded her arms across her chest,
> And couched her head upon her breast,
> And looked askance at Christabel—
> Jesu, Maria, shield her well!
> A snake's small eye blinks dull and shy;
> And the lady's eyes they shrunk in her head,
> Each shrunk up to a serpent's eye,
> And with somewhat of malice, and more of dread,
> At Christabel she looked askance!—[84]

Under the spell of the serpent-like Geraldine, Christabel assumes characteristics of the serpent, such as hissing and a look of "dull and treacherous hate!" Geraldine's evil power has gained control, at least, momentarily. The poem, unfortunately, was never completed. It would have been interesting to know the final outcome of the struggle between innocence and malevolence.

In an embittered and cynical tone, Byron uses the serpent to symbolize the hatred of a mother for her hunchback son. Bertha rejects the name of mother, feeling that it is not fit for one who by some unnatural act gave birth to a monster like Arnold, "As foolish hens at times hatch vipers, by/Sitting upon strange eggs."[85] Arnold, suffering from his mother's hate, in turn hates himself and all others. When he wounds himself, knowing that he is ugly and unnatural and unlike creatures more fortunate, he wishes that each drop of blood which falls to earth "Would rise a snake to sting them, as they have stung me![86] The hate of a mother for a son multiplies and spreads with the vehemence and rapidity of a pestilence. Like a neglected wound which spreads its poison over the body, hatred becomes pervasive and general, contaminating all that it touches.

Blake also uses the serpent to symbolize horrible familial relationships. Tiriel, cast out into the world by ungrateful, ravenous sons, speaks of them as " 'Serpents, not sons, wreathing around the bones of Tiriel!' "[87] Throughout the poem, the old blind father can think of his sons only as greedy and ravaging reptiles crawling over the face of the earth and spilling their venom.

In his dramatization of the Cain-Abel story, Blake uses the serpent to symbolize murder—the height of enmity in familial relations. Preparing to bury Abel, Adam hears Jehovah call to him. Remembering the curse which God put on both man and serpent in the Garden of Eden, the grief-stricken father expresses his hostility and bitterness:

> It is in vain. I will not hear thee
> Henceforth! Is this thy Promise, that
> the Woman's Seed
> Should bruise the Serpent's head? Is
> this the Serpent?[88]

Shelley also presents the serpent in an image treating of murder. The slaves, slaying men who tried to save them, are like snakes returning harm for benefit:

> Like rabid snakes, that sting some gentle child
> Who brings them food, when winter false
> and fair
> Allures them forth with its cold smiles, so
> wild
> They rage among the camp.[89]

Enmity among men takes on appalling dimensions when gratitude is repaid with ingratitude, kindness with unkindness, and love with hate. The world is in a deplorable condition, indeed, when those not deserving murder are murdered.

In Shelley's poem *Ginevra*, dealing with the unhappiness of a bride who steals forth from the marriage festivities to listen to the reproaches of her former lover, the serpent symbolizes any unsympathetic or malicious opposition to love. Ginevra gives a rather comprehensive survey of those things which could possibly change love between man and woman:

> "Friend, if earthly violence or ill,
> Suspicion, doubt, or the tyrannic will
> Of parents, chance or custom, time or change,
> Or circumstance, or terror, or revenge,
> Or wildered looks, or words, or evil speech,
> With all their stings and venom, can impeach
> Our love,—we love not."[90]

Those forces which Ginevra labels as viperous and destructive to her own personal love are equally destructive to a more philosophical love among mankind. Ginevra's idealistic statement that true love can withstand serpent evils is a clear expression of Shelley's faith. The poet depicts destruction as a snake, held in check by aspects of love:

> Gentleness, Virtue, Wisdom, and Endurance,
> These are the seals of that most firm assurance
>       Which bars the pit over Destruction's strength;
> And if, with infirm hand, Eternity,
> Mother of many acts and hours, should free
>       The serpent that would clasp her with his length;
> These are the spells by which to reassume
> An empire o'er the disentangled doom.[91]

## Literary Criticism

There is another area under the category "Man Against Man" especially meaningful to the imaginative and creative poet—literary criticism. The serpent as symbol of literary criticism deals with the extended meaning of the word "criticism"—faultfinding. To an artist who relies upon divine inspiration, a critic is often considered a viper, dealing a death blow to many of his productions. The temperamental, emotional, interpretative poets often fall prey to the cold, logical, and analytical evaluations of the critics. These critics are more often than not individuals who are earth-bound and never soar in the rarefied atmosphere of beautiful poetic expression. The habit of the critic to inflict harm is a viperous quality, according to the creative poet, especially the romantic creative poet.

Illustrative of this antagonism between the imaginative poet and the unimaginative critic is Shelley's denunciation of the unappreciative reviewers of Keats's *Endymion*. Feeling that such harshness had caused the poet's death, Shelley compares the critics to hungry dragons and serpents emerging from their dens to devour the young poet. The grieved Shelley, speaking through Urania, asks the spirit of Keats:

> "Why didst thou leave the trodden paths of men
> Too soon, and with weak hands though mighty heart
> Dare the unpastured dragon in his den?
> Defenceless as thou wert, oh, where was then
> Wisdom the mirrored shield, or scorn the spear?"[92]

Shelley regretted that Keats was sensitive to, and hurt by, the criticism. He wished that the young poet had scorned and rejected the reviewers as Byron had done. Byron's crippling blast at the bards and reviewers reminds Shelley of Apollo's fatal blow at the Python:

> "... how they fled
> When like Apollo, from his golden bow
> The Pythian of the age one arrow sped
> And smiled."[93]

Continuing with the image of the critics as serpents, Shelley compares Keats to the sun, whose light attracts the loathsome creatures, providing for them the opportunity to spawn, that is, to produce their criticism:

> "The sun comes forth, and many reptiles spawn;
> He sets, and each ephemeral insect then
> Is gathered into death without a dawn,
> And the immortal stars awake again;
> So is it in the world of living men:
> A godlike mind soars forth, in its delight

> Making earth bare and veiling heaven, and when
> It sinks, the swarms that dimmed or shared
>    its light
> Leave to its kindred lamps the spirit's awful night."[94]

It is only when a great mind appears that the viperous critics can spawn. Their criticisms dimming the light shed by the great mind, the critics destroy the only thing which enables them to produce. Their source of light gone, they sit in a world of darkness. Bitterly reproaching the *Quarterly* critic for his infamy, Shelley exhorts him to know himself for what he is, "And ever at thy season be thou free/To spill the venom when thy fangs o'erflow."[95]

In a lighter vein, Shelley chided Mary as being critic- or viper-bitten when she objected to *The Witch of Atlas* because of its lack of moral or human interest. She wished that Shelley would treat more substantial subjects rather than those of a visionary nature. The poet observes the paradoxical nature of the critic in that he can kill though he is dead:

> How, my dear Mary,—are you critic-bitten
>    (For vipers kill, though dead) by some review,
> That you condemn these verses I have written
> Because they tell no story, false or true?[96]

Lacking imagination and evaluating only on the basis of whether or not a poem tells a story, the negative literary critics are even worse than dead serpents because they have the power to strip not only the poets but also their poetry of life.

## Institutions Against Man

### Kings and Kingcraft

Opposed to all forces weakening or destroying man's strength as both a divine and human being, Blake vents his anger many times against kings and priests, considering them as man's most formidable foes. The terms "king" and "priest" signify any despot or tyrant attempting to subjugate man. Blake believed that the individual must exercise his intuition and heed the inner light if he is to participate in the spiritual harmony of the universe.

External distractions simply take a man off-center and leave him without anchor. Any external restraint, restriction, or imposition thwarts man in his effort to remain part of the eternal world, and since his only chance to share the spiritual harmony lies within himself, then yielding to the decrees and impositions of institutions is fatal. Reliance upon his intuition precludes conformity and obeisance to any form of tyranny.

Blake's poetry expounds the belief that the mind can apprehend truth immediately. The senses grasp only the perceivable, visible world. They miss the real and absolute world, which only intuition, man's most powerful faculty, can reach. Therefore, Blake remonstrates against any restrictions prohibiting the expression and exercise of all faculties, particularly intuition. Among these restrictions and restraints is the tyranny of kings and priests, whose decrees are designed to bridle man's native impulses and passions. Repressed native impulses and passions are simply a condition of negation, which to Blake is passiveness and a sin. On the other hand, energy is the life-force, active and virtuous. Paralyzed into submission and inertia, man is only part human. Liberated to express every facet of his personality, he is a total human being, whom Blake equates with the divine, as opposed to the fractional man, who exercises only his senses and thus falls to the level of a serpent. Blake interprets kings and priests in their institutionalism and despotism as preventing expression of the whole man.

In a Blakean sense, Shelley associates tyrants, kings, and priests in the same class—all sly and treacherous like the snake. The foul tyrant summoned the kings and priests who

> knew his cause their own and swore
> Like wolves and serpents to their mutual wars
> Strange truce.[97]

Shelley presents kings and subjects as natural foes. The power of a king, like a pestilence, pollutes whatever it touches and man's obedience to such polluted power makes him a slave.

Mythology provides an interesting background for the association of kings and snakes. Beginning with Zeus, chief of the Olympians, mythological kings often assumed the forms of serpents. Kings at Delphi and Thebes are supposed to have transformed themselves into serpents in order to kill their predecessors and reign for a time in their stead. The hypothesis that these kings of Thebes and Delphi had as their sacred animal the serpent or dragon derives some support from the legend that Cadmus and Harmonia left Thebes as serpents to rule over a tribe of Eel-men. Frazer repeats the legend that the Athenians kept a sacred serpent on the Acropolis and fed it with honey-cakes; it was identified with Erichthonius (or Erectheus), one of the ancient kings of Athens.[98] Cecrops, the first king of Athens, is said to have been half-man and half-serpent, the lower part of his body lying in coils. Cychreus gained the kingdom of Salamis by slaying a snake, but after his own death reappeared in the form of a reptile. These and many other stories constitute a formidable tradition that kings assumed the disguise of serpents and that often after death their spirits transmigrated into the bodies of serpents.

In his poem about the French Revolution, Blake paints a chilling picture of a king who adamantly holds on to his power and is jealously guarded by fawning and hissing serpents:

> The cold newt,
> And snake, and damp toad on the kingly foot
> crawl, or croak on the awful knee,
> Shedding their slime, in folds of the robe
> the crown'd adder builds and hisses
> From stony brows.[99]

Even though the king is being threatened by the revolutionary forces in France, he clings tenaciously to his throne, receiving support only from the cold, creeping, croaking, and hissing creatures. Inside the robe are both the king and adder, which also wears a white spot on its head and, thus, appears to be crowned. Both wield an evil power and hiss their defiance at the world. The phrase "stony brows" refers not only to the hard, cold brow of the king or the unyielding crown resting on his head but also to the brow and crown of the adder. The adder in ancient times was reputed to have a stone in its head.

The deafness of the adder is a quality which Byron finds suitable for describing the rulers of the city-state Florence in their imperious and unyielding banishment and punishment of Dante, who still pleads love for his city:

> ... I would have gather'd thee
> Beneath a parent pinion, hadst thou heard
> My voice; but as the adder, deaf and fierce,
> Against the breast that cherish'd thee was
>     stirred
> Thy venom, and my state thou didst amerce,
> And doom this body forfeit to the fire.[100]

Byron's image of the deaf adder suggests the Biblical description of the adder which stops its ears so that it cannot be charmed or enchanted.

Not only the adder but also the asp, basilisk, and cockatrice are used by the Romantic poets to suggest the deadly power of kings. The word "basilisk" means "a little king," a title gained because of not only a crown-like white spot on its head but also because of the deference which other snakes paid it, according to mythological legends. Whatever other snakes were doing, even if eating a sumptuous meal, they withdrew when the "king of serpents" hissed to announce his approach. There were different varieties of this monarch, but all were capable of wreaking destruction. Some killed by casting a fatal glance, others destroyed by emitting a deadly vapor, another made flesh fall mysteriously from the victim's bones, and another could kill with a sting of its tail. This belief in its extraordinary potency to bring a victim to destruction marks it as a symbol of unapproachable power. The basilisk is more often represented as killing with a blast of breath, and the cockatrice with a fatal glance of its evil eye, but generally the Romantic poets use them interchangeably.

Coleridge prompts his character Tallien to compare the tyrant kings of Europe with cockatrices, spreading a pestilence upon all the Continent. Tallien, aware of Robespierre's ambition to tyrannize in the name of freedom, knows that France will be no better off under his rule. Tallien poses France's dilemma in this question:

> Is it for this we wage eternal war
> Against the tyrant horde of murderers,

> The crownéd cockatrices whose foul venom
> Infects all Europe?[101]

A cockatrice leaving death and destruction in its wake as it crawls about the country is no more dangerous than the kings emitting a deadly venom from their thrones.

An intriguing concept to lovers of freedom is that kings frequently secrete serpents in the folds of their robes, hug them to their breasts, and give them warmth and protection. When George IV entered Dublin in triumph within ten days after Queen Caroline's death, Byron felt that Ireland must no longer boast of being rid of reptiles. The poet exhorts:

> . . . let her long-boasted proverb be hush'd
> Which proclaims that from Erin no reptile
> can spring—
> See the cold-blooded serpent, with venom
> full flush'd,
> Still warming its folds in the breast of
> a king![102]

Ireland's boast that she had no snakes is, of course, a reference to the legend of Saint Patrick. The Saint is usually represented expelling serpents and other reptiles from the island with his pastoral staff or by holding a shamrock leaf. With George's appearance, Ireland's boast became an empty one: A serpent under the auspices of a king had re-entered.

Byron also associates a tyrannical government with the Hydra, a fabulous serpent of many heads and with prodigious ability to multiply. Expressing Byron's thoughts, Marino Faliero, a democratic Doge of Venice, compares the aristocracy in power to a Hydra which has been permitted to survive and to multiply its evils until it has corrupted all of Venice. So when the talented and courageous Doge is accorded many honors and asked if he would like to be king, he agrees, provided the people of Venice will share his sovereignty,

> So that nor they nor I were further slaves
> To this o'ergrown aristocratic Hydra,
> The poisonous heads of whose envenom'd body
> Have breathed a pestilence upon us all.[103]

The democratic Doge considers political tyranny a many-headed serpent monster. Cutting off one head results in the appearance of two new heads; riddance of one evil in the aristocracy does not insure against a multiplication of evil deeds. Aware that cutting off the head does not eradicate the trouble, the Doge advises: "I tell you, you must strike, and suddenly,/Full to the Hydra's heart—its head will follow."[104] In the same vein, Calendaro, knowing of the evils of the aristocratic rulers, says that they deserve

> such pity
> As when the viper hath been cut to pieces
> The separate fragments quivering in the sun
> In the last energy of venomous life.[105]

The destructive power of the coil of a serpent often symbolizes the formidable power residing in a king's crown. Just as the serpent's greatest power of attack lies within its coil, so does a king's most formidable power lie within his coronal. Wordsworth's poem *Dion* illustrates this particular serpent symbolism. Dion, the virtuous and honest son of Dionysius, an evil and degenerate man, falls victim to his father's plots. Seeing one day a woman resembling one of the Furies, Dion senses impending misfortune —which does turn out to be the suicide of his son—and orders the spectre out of his sight: " '—let me rather see/The coronal that coiling vipers make.' "[106] Plagued and beset by the evils attendant upon his father's lust for power as king of Sicily, Dion realizes that a tyrant's coronal is as potentially dangerous as a serpent's coil.

Hatred of institutional tyranny, as exhibited by kings and monarchs, led Shelley to denounce in *Ode to Liberty* even the name "king," which should be written in the sand and, like a serpent's trail, blown away by the slightest stir of air. A lover of freedom and a staunch believer in the right of man to exercise his native impulses and desires rather than live according to the decrees of kings and other rulers, Shelley says that even though the word "king" is short and weak, it has the power to wield

iron instruments inspiring fear in man and exacting deference.
The poet exhorts free men:

> Lift the victory-flashing sword,
> And cut the snaky knots of this foul gordian word,
> Which, weak itself as stubble, yet can bind
> Into a mass, irrefragably firm,
> The axes and the rods which awe mankind;
> The sound has poison in it, 'tis the sperm
> Of what makes life foul, cankerous, and abhorred.[107]

## Priests and Priestcraft

When the Romantic poets, particularly the mystics Blake and
Shelley, denounce kings and priests, they are denouncing all op-
pressors and autocrats in the spheres of government or religion.
Innately noble and reliable, man can govern himself. Possessing
a divine nature and the faculty of intuition, he is entitled to his
own conception and interpretation of God; therefore, the Romanticists, having faith in the individual, refused to embrace an
institutionalized God, based on the concepts of others. Blake and
Shelley, particularly, felt that they could conceive the image of
God and needed no priestly interpreters, who superimposed
upon God their own limitations and biases. Priests, ministers,
and rabbis then—interpreters of rigid, orthodox religions—were
not acceptable.

One of the earliest instances in which ecclesiastics are denounced as serpents for their hypocritical presumptuousness as
spokesmen for God occurs in the New Testament. Jesus ad-
monishes the scribes and Pharisees to practice what they preach,
or to set good examples rather than hypocritically preach about
them: "*Ye* serpents, *ye* generation of vipers, how can ye escape
the damnation of hell?"[108] Christ's denunciation of the Pharisees
as vipers may be Blake and Shelley's heritage for their use of
serpents as symbols of priestcraft.

Blake's serpent is nearly always attired in rich and dazzling
gems. This attractive external appearance disguising the evil
within the serpent may be suggestive of the outward trappings

and elaborate rites hiding the impurity of the priestcraft. Blake may be expressing this parallelism in the following poem:

> I saw a chapel all of gold
> That none did dare to enter in,
> And many weeping stood without,
> Weeping, mourning, worshipping.
> I saw a serpent rise between
> The white pillars of the door,
> And he forc'd & forc'd & forc'd,
> Down the golden hinges tore.
> And along the pavement sweet,
> Set with pearls & rubies bright,
> All his slimy length he drew,
> Till upon the altar white
> Vomiting his poison out
> On the bread & on the wine.
> So I turn'd into a sty
> And laid me down among the swine.[109]

The "chapel all of gold," the "golden hinges," and the pavement "Set with pearls & rubies bright"—all symbolize the priests' love of exhibitionism and material splendor. They attempt to persuade man to accept them as authorities and interpreters of God's word. That the serpent "forced" the door open suggests the despotism of the priestcraft in imposing upon man those ethical and moral codes antithetical to his natural impulses and passions. Religion then becomes a special bailiwick of the priests, who tyrannize over the multitudes.

Reminiscent of Blake's association of the priestcraft with the serpent in their attempt to impose restrictions and beguile man into an acceptance of error, Shelley describes an Iberian priest:

> ... for in his breast
> Did hate and guile lie watchful, intertwined,
> Twin serpents in one deep and winding nest.[110]

One of Shelley's most shocking serpent images protesting the evils of institutions is that comparing organized religion to a python. Reminiscing to Rosalind about Lionel's visions of faith and hope which he saw blasted, Helen names Power and Faith as two of man's enemies. The Christian creed, like a wounded python, still manages to move among men, trampling and deceiving them:

> Gray Power was seated
> Safely on her ancestral throne;
> And Faith, the Python, undefeated,
> Even to its blood-stained steps dragged on
> Her foul and wounded train.[111]

Blake was opposed to a tyrannical God and to tyrannical representatives of God. Blake could accept only a God of mercy, pity, and love; therefore, he must reject any spokesman who represents God as a cruel and destructive monster and who threatens to let loose a plague of horrible diseases and other misfortunes on man. In *Vala, or The Four Zoas,* the poet envisions a serpent setting himself up as the representative and spokesman of God, who, he says, made him in the image of man and appointed him to be the custodian and distributor of diseases to be used as curses in troubled times:

> The Prester Serpent runs
> Among the ranks, crying, "Listen to the Priest
> of God, ye warriors;
> "This Cowl upon my head he plac'd in times of
> Everlasting,
> "And said, 'Go forth & guide my battles; like
> the jointed spine
> " 'Of Man I made thee when I blotted Man from
> life and light
> " 'Take thou the Seven Diseases of Man; store
> them for times to come
> " 'In storehouses, in secret places that I will
> tell thee of,
> " 'To be my great & awful curses at the time
> appointed.' "[112]

Blake's choice of title for a serpent who presumes to speak for God is significant. The word "prester" means "priest" or "venomous serpent," and may point back to Prester John, a legendary priest and king of the Middle Ages, who was a lover of wealth, power, and conquest.

Shelley, too, denounces the hypocrisy of God's self-appointed representatives, who pretend to be disciples of mercy and charity and beguile man with their venomous lies. *The Revolt of Islam* is a narrative of oppression, a condition enslaving and debasing man. And among these oppressions, which man is attempting to throw off, are the "religious frauds by which they have been deluded into submission."[113] Shelley is impatient with priests who frighten man into submission by presenting God as an unmerciful tyrant, eager to punish souls and, thus, feed His wrath. In *The Revolt of Islam*, the priests present God as a wrathful God, waiting for Judgment Day to come; but, in the meantime, the priests, presuming to appease the wrath of God until Judgment Day, gather human souls for the devils of hell. Thus, they present God as unmerciful and sadistic, intent on making sure that man has no respite from suffering:

> And Priests rushed through their ranks, some
> counterfeiting
> The rage they did inspire, some mad indeed
> With their own lies; they said their god was
> waiting
> To see his enemies writhe, and burn, and bleed,
> And that till then, the snakes of Hell had need
> Of human souls:—three hundred furnaces
> Soon blazed through the wide City, where, with
> speed,
> Men brought their infidel kindred to appease
> God's wrath, and while they burned, knelt round on
> quivering knees.[114]

Shelley felt that many crimes are committed in the name of religion. Afraid of a punitive God, as the priests represent Him, man descends into a groveling form. To Shelley and Blake, only a God who encourages man's natural dignity and divinity is acceptable, and this God is the quintessence of mercy, forgiveness, and love.

In *Milton*, Blake again uses the serpent to symbolize hypocritical priestcraft. Satan himself is now presented as a priest. Leutha, having lost her spiritual nature and become a captive

of the senses and materialism, acknowledges herself as a priestess
in the service of Satan, the high priest, who is

> Cloth'd in the Serpent's folds, in selfish
>     holiness demanding purity
> Being most impure.[115]

Satan and the priests are hypocrites in that they avow holiness
but are unholy. They punish and are destructive to man's eternal
spirit. Orthodox ethical and moral codes demand the impossible,
turn people into hypocrites, punish their failures, and then extend
the cloak of mercy, which is an act of purity to cover impurities.
Man is forced outwardly to conform while inwardly the spark of
divine light gutters and fails. The less light man has within his
soul, the more he tries to impose his narrow and constricting
ideas upon others.

As a priestess in the service of the high priest Satan, Leutha
describes her own acts as the stings of the serpent. Like priests
and serpents, Satan and Leutha do harm while pretending benefit.
Leutha analyzes her evil power:

> To do unkind things in kindness, with power arm'd
>     to say
> The most irritating things in the midst of tears
>     and love,
> These are the stings of the Serpent.[116]

The phrase "serpent temples" occurs rather frequently in
Blake's poetry. A temple, or church, artificial and of material
splendor, is the manifestation of God as apprehended by reason
and the senses of man embracing a materialistic world:

> The Serpent Temples thro' the Earth,
>     from the wide Plain of Salisbury,
> Resound with cries of Victims.[117]

Such temples belong to religions that are formulated by self-appointed spokesmen of God, who victimize and imprison man
rather than liberate him. The word "temple" refers also to castles

of kings, who like the priests, stress the wordly and temporal rather than the spiritual and eternal:

> In thoughts perturb'd they rose from the bright
> ruins, silent following
> The fiery King, who sought his ancient temple,
> serpent-form'd,
> That stretches out its shady length along the
> Island white.[118]

The phrase "serpent-form'd" means a temple formed or built by serpent-like priests and kings and in this particular image may also suggest the sprawling length of the king's castle. In their desire to dazzle and subjugate man, government and religious institutions emphasize elaborate physical expression of an impoverished spiritual condition.

Blake's words when he was approaching death are a terse and accurate summary of the attitude of the Romantic poets toward any institution denying the individual the opportunity to govern his own thoughts and actions. Writing to a friend about the death of another friend, Blake philosophizes:

> "Flaxman is Gone, & we must All soon follow, every one to his Own Eternal House, Leaving the delusive Goddess Nature & her Laws, to get into Freedom from all Law of the Members, into The Mind, in which every one is King & Priest in his own House."[119]

Recognizing life as the time when the physical is in control, Blake envisions death as man's liberator. The spirit, liberated from the body and its subjection to delusive forces, becomes its own king and priest. This is the only concept of king and priest which the Romanticists—notably Blake and Shelley—could accept.

# V

## Summary and Conclusions

$A$ STUDY OF THE SERPENT'S ROLE in the imagery and symbolism of the major Romantic poets provides a surprisingly complete and accurate picture of the significant characteristics of the Romantic movement. No animal could have represented more adequately than does the serpent both the sensuous and spiritual worlds not only of man but also of all of nature.

The intuitive imagination of the Romanticists discovered a whole new world of nature and man, both of them vibrant with life. Shedding the old skin of eighteenth-century restraints and restrictions, the Romanticists began life anew, revolted against the old and stagnant, wound their way in and out of the natural world, and discovered the supernatural, mythological, and spiritual worlds. Their eagerness to delight in the senses, to nourish their spirit, to reclaim their kinship with animal and plant life— in fact their curiosity to rediscover themselves and a lost world— explains the vibrancy of their imagery, especially powerful in its visual, tactile, and kinesthetic appeal. The imagery of the Romantic poetry, like the poets themselves, pulsates with movement, color, and eagerness. The symbolism of Romantic poetry is as abundant and varied as its imagery. Symbolic interpretations of Romanticism are mirrored in the symbolic interpretations of the serpent. In brief, a study of serpent imagery and serpent symbolism in Romanticism provides a survey of the outstanding characteristics of Romanticism.

Serpent imagery in the major English Romantic poets—Blake, Wordsworth, Coleridge, Byron, Shelley, and Keats—may be classified into six categories: the serpent compared with man's emotions; with man's physical and mental attributes; with the whole man; with areas and aspects of human life and experiences; with natural phenomena and man-made objects; and, finally, the serpent presented as mere animal or as pictorial detail.[1]

Conclusions in reference to the number of serpent images in the major Romantic poets are meaningful in terms of their complete works. Listed in the order of quantity of total work produced, Wordsworth and Byron are first, then Shelley and Blake, next Coleridge, and last Keats. Although Wordsworth is probably the most voluminous of these writers, he has relatively few serpent images. Shelley has the greatest number, Blake and Byron are next, Coleridge follows, and then come Keats and Wordsworth.

Shelley not only has the greatest number of serpent images but also uses the serpent in the widest gamut of meaning. Shelley emphasizes no one image category and is well represented in all six of them. This multivariate distribution is not surprising when one remembers Shelley's use of the serpent to represent opposites and his ability to reconcile irreconcilables. The six classifications selected best fit Shelley's poetry. His serpent has movement and visual appeal but is achromatic rather than chromatic.

Blake has the second largest number of serpent images. His poetry yields many images for the category depicting the whole man as viperous. Because of the highly symbolic nature of his poetry, an abundance of his images are also pure pictorial detail when considered only for their overt and stated meaning. His interest in art doubtlessly accounts for superiority in pictorial detail. Blake stresses visual appeal even more than Shelley does and nearly always presents the serpent richly attired in brilliant colors. The colors, however, are used artificially. Rather than present the serpent with variegated skin, Blake depicts it as studded with rare, resplendent gems and stones and wearing a crest of fire. Blake's serpent exhibits violent, exaggerated movements: It is monstrous, lashes its tail, catapults through the heavens and abysses, and in general moves as if being hurled by some external or outside force. Generally his serpent is combative and seems to participate in crises of cosmic proportions. Even though he deplores the lamentable condition to which the senses reduce man, Blake places great emphasis on sensuous images. His serpent is nearly always sensuous and greedy.

Byron's poetry yields the third largest number of serpent images. The poet uses the serpent frequently to portray man and areas and aspects of human life and experiences. Few of his serpent images fall into the categories of natural phenomena and pictorial detail. Byron's interest in social activities is reflected in his dramas. Because the serpent is conspicuous in his dramas, one gets the feeling that Byron's serpent is human—erect and speaking. His serpent is emphasized for its venom and sting more than for color and muscular movement.

Coleridge emphasizes the serpent to characterize the whole man but disregards the serpent in his descriptions of natural phenomena. The poet often uses the serpent in his dramas, where the characters, like Byron's particularly, call one another serpents. Coleridge also emphasizes the snake's evil eye, a highly dramatic attribute, which the poet himself was proud of possessing. Generally Coleridge's snakes are colorless. A notable exception is the beautiful water-snake scene in *The Rime of the Ancient Mariner.* When one remembers this colorful description and the "bright green snake" in *Christabel,* he is inclined to characterize Coleridge's serpent as colorful, but generally this is not true.

Keats's poetry yields serpent images for all classifications, though the serpent is almost never used to describe areas and aspects of human life and experiences. Not concerned with social problems but with the questions of sensuous delight and beauty, Keats stresses the brilliant color and writhing movement of the serpent. This emphasis gives the serpent sensuous appeal, so vivid that the poet's delight is easily captured. A perfect example of this infectious delight is *Lamia,* the most extensive Romantic poem having serpent imagery at the core.

Wordsworth's serpent images reveal a strong interest in natural phenomena. Few of his serpent images deal with emotions, and areas and aspects of human life and experiences. Wordsworth's poetry pays tribute to the trees, flowers, mountains, lakes, and valleys and creates a quiet, tranquil mood. The serpent is not usually part of this mood. But when the serpent does participate in a scene of innocence, harmony, and love, the result is a magnificent portrayal of Wordsworth's pantheistic doctrine.

Symbolism is difficult to classify because of its highly interpretative character. It is understandable that symbolism, which deals with esoteric meaning, is more difficult to classify than imagery, which deals with exoteric meaning. Like serpent imagery, however, serpent symbolism can be broken down into acceptable categories. The specific problem was to decide which symbolic interpretations of the serpent are primary and which are secondary. For example, the same serpent image can be interpreted as symbolic of imagination, pantheism, or sexuality. Sexuality is not used as a category in this dissertation. T. R. Henn, however, in *The Apple and the Spectroscope* does include it, at least as a subcategory under the breakdown he suggests: traditional, personal, archetypal, and Freudian.

There are many ways one could classify serpent images according to the symbolism interpreted. Here they are divided into five categories: the serpent as symbol of idealism (imagination, benevolence, pantheism); as symbol of the Fall of Man (serpent as beguiler, woman as serpent-beguiler); as symbol of materialism (analytic reason, empiricism, sensuousness); as symbol of man against man (enmity, literary criticism); and as symbol of institutions against man (kingcraft, priestcraft). All the images are not classified symbolically, but representative images are discussed in each category. Conclusions drawn about serpent symbolism begin with general statements about the category and continue with references to the individual poets.

It is not surprising that the category "Idealism" reveals a significant role of the serpent. Being idealists, the Romanticists discredit the visible world about them and by the use of their imagination penetrate a visionary world of truth, beauty, and goodness. What more effective way of expressing faith in a better world than by presenting the most sinful of animals as sinless, beautiful, and divine? Here, Shelley makes the most significant use of the serpent as symbol of this idealistic world. This is not surprising when one observes that Shelley gives the serpent the widest range of meaning and is most successful in reconciling irreconcilables. Wordsworth, the great nature-lover and believer in the participation of all life in the all-pervading divinity, is rather prominent in this category. Keats, the apostle of beauty, also recognizes the serpent as contributing to the good of the world. Coleridge and Blake, however, nearly always present the snake as evil and, therefore, generally exclude it from their ideal worlds. Byron's serpent in many instances is admirable for its retaliatory nature but can hardly be recognized as benevolent. Neither Byron nor his serpent ever turned the other cheek.

The category "The Fall of Man" discloses significant comments on the poets and their beliefs and attitudes. Byron and Blake are the most concerned with man's banishment from heaven and are reluctant to forget the serpent's alleged crime in the Garden of Eden. These two poets build many images on the concept of the serpent as beguiler. Byron, Shelley, and Keats present woman as a convert of the serpent and equally adept in the art of tempting man. Blake, however, generally presents man as a serpent lusting for power, possessions, and woman; he does not generally represent woman herself as the serpent-tempter of man. Coleridge is aware of the association between the serpent as a beguiler and woman as a serpent-beguiler, but his most famous example is that of a woman bewitching another woman rather than a man. Woman as a serpent-beguiler does not appear in Wordsworth's poetry.

It is natural that the category "Materialism" brings into the foreground the poet so dissatisfied with the condition of man and the perceptual world that he cannot forget for long the causes of such sordidness. Blake is by far the most outspoken opponent of materialism and its sources—analytic reason, empiricism, and sensuousness. This may be in part due to his closeness to the eighteenth century and its emphasis on rationalism and the senses. Blake cannot see any spiritual value in nature; it is materialistic and deceives man into an acceptance of the material. To some degree, Shelley and Coleridge deplore materialism and its aspects but do not use the serpent to symbolize this philosophy to the great extent that Blake does. At times, Wordsworth also deplores the "meddling intellect" but not in terms of the serpent. Byron, though often rationalistic and sensuous, does not express himself in this area. Keats at times complains about analytic reason but generally does not concern himself with this problem.

The category "Man Against Man" gives insight into the major Romantic poets and their concern with tyranny and injustice among individuals. All the poets use expressions denoting enmity among men. In their poetry, one of the most frequently hurled invectives among enemies is "you viper" or "you serpent." Favorite derogatory descriptions are "a venomous tongue," "an evil eye," "a defiling breath like that of the basilisk," "envenomed fangs," "a stinging tail," *ad infinitum*. The serpent more than any other animal is used to describe malevolent human beings or to express hatred among men. Shelley's serpent images denouncing literary critics are interesting examples of a poet's proclivity to reduce unpleasant men to the level of serpents. Byron, Shelley, and Coleridge use the serpent most frequently to describe the enmity between individual men. Blake, particularly in his prophetic poems, appears to be presenting enmity between individual men, but in reality the enmity is between philosophical and psychological systems. For example, he personifies the struggle between the spiritual and the physical, the intuitive and the rational, and the infinite and the finite.

The category "Institutions Against Man" gives a glimpse into all the poets except Keats, who was preoccupied with worlds of mythology and beauty. Kings and kingcraft at one time or another are denounced by Blake, Byron, Shelley, Coleridge, and Wordsworth. Priests and priestcraft are attacked vehemently only by Blake and Shelley. Coleridge implies a denunciation of priests in one image. By "priest," he means any man holding a scourge of power in one hand and the Bible in the other. Blake and Shelley are the most vociferous in their protests. Constantly upholding the right of the individual to give expression to his own impulses, thoughts, and convictions, these two poets are relentless in their attacks against the serpentine restraints of institutions.

Literature and art, in general, are abundant in symbols because the creative man is aware of the conflict between conscious and unconscious forces. He realizes that man must reconcile the antagonism between these opposites in order to achieve unity and harmony within himself and with the universe. This reconciliation requires an expression of both the conscious and unconscious. The unconscious does not express itself by words but can be recognized only through symbols. These symbols, however, do not always mean the same thing to every individual. Ambivalent attitudes prevail between individuals and within each individual. This ambivalence explains the multiple and opposite interpretations of the same symbol.

And one of the most provocative symbols is the serpent. Wingfield Digby discusses the significance of the serpent, which, like all powerful symbols, contains within itself its own opposite. This quality makes the symbol difficult for analytic reason but easy for the intuitive imagination to apprehend. This author observes:

> The serpent is primarily the symbol of the infinite locked up in the finite; the image of the misconception of the part as the whole. The finite thinks it can contain and comprehend the infinite, the part the whole. So long as there is this thought, this misconception, the serpent is the subtle deceiver. Or stated in kinetic psychological terms, the libido or life-energy is the great tempter.[2]

The six major English Romantic poets found the serpent an extremely interesting symbol in their efforts to probe the unconscious and give to themselves and the world a better understanding of the meaning of life.

Blake, the harbinger of Romanticism, was a man of many talents and interests. He was an engraver, painter, poet, and mystic with a keen interest in religion, psychology, and philosophy. Blake is an outstanding poet of symbols, and throughout his works he uses the serpent to symbolize materialism and rationalism, antagonists of the spiritual world. He is a visionary who abhors any and all unfair authorities.

Wordsworth, the poet of the universal and everyday world of landscape and nature, spoke clearly of nature's tranquilizing and ennobling influence and revived an interest in mythology. Originally rebellious against shams and injustices of the man-made world, Wordsworth, the pantheist, became in his declining years more orthodox and traditional. His serpent plays no momentous roles and engages in no heroic actions and, like the poet himself, is generally peaceful and calm.

Psychologist, metaphysician, and scholar, Coleridge had a strong interest in the strange and supernatural. With the use of the serpent and the help of his unconscious, he conjures up at times the fantastic and magical. The serpent is valuable to Coleridge the literary critic, also. He uses the serpent in his definition of a legitimate poem, which carries the reader along smoothly and pleasurably from one idea to another, each idea containing the power to move the reader to the next idea: "Like the motion of a serpent, . . . at every step he pauses and half recedes, and from the retrogressive movement collects the force which again carries him onward."[3]

Forceful and sweeping, Byron with an all-too-realistic understanding of humanity was both a rationalist and a romanticist. Generally, he was a romanticist of his own age rather than a past age, a poet of humankind. Byron was sentimental and cynical, romantic and retaliatory, humorous and satirical. Often pessimistic and incisive, but usually buoyant, he endowed his serpent with the same qualities.

A confirmed poet of revolt, Shelley was idealistic and mystical. His poetry often creates an ephemeral and ethereal world, growing out of imagination, intuition, and feeling. His imagery is outstanding and all in all his symbolism is the most balanced, inclusive, and varied of the major Romantic poets. Shelley's serpents run the gamut from good to evil, from spiritual to physical, and from the plain, ordinary snake to the fabulous amphisbaena, which appears to have two heads and to move in both directions at the same time.

Keats, the apostle of beauty, lived in the worlds of mythology and sense appeal. His imagery is sensuous and radiantly alive. Eager to present the object itself, Keats submerges his own personality in his exquisite description and enables the reader to get the feel of things. Among the many objects he focuses upon in his poetry is the serpent in one form or another.

These biographical sketches of Keats and the other Romanticists and their serpents are a meaningful glimpse into the whole Romantic movement, which Douglas Bush summarizes beautifully:

> The Romantic movement involved.. a change from a mechanical conception of the world to an enthusiastic religion of nature, from rational virtue to emotional sensibility, from Hobbesian egoism to humanitarian benevolence, from realism to optimism, from acceptance of things as they are to faith in progress, from contentment with urban civilization to sentimental primitivism, from traditional doctrines of literary imitation to conceptions of the naive and original, from poetic preoccupation with the normal, the true, and the actual to dreams of the strange, the beautiful and the ideal.[4]

Vibrating with the spirit of revolt, the major English Romantic poets and their movement provide an abundance of serpent imagery and symbolism. An examination of this serpent imagery and symbolism makes the "collegiate philosopher's" assertion that the serpent was the "founder of Romanticism" seem less of an exaggeration.

# Notes and References

# Notes and References

## Chapter One

1. The position outlined here is that taken by the Romanticists themselves. It can be pointed out with considerable justification that the revolutionary ideas of human freedom and death to the tyrant espoused by the Romantic poets were expressed in the eighteenth century by many writers, though seldom in poetry. In France, one could list Voltaire, Rousseau, Diderot and the Encyclopedists; and in Great Britain and America, Samuel Johnson, Swift, Goldsmith, Robert Burns, Hogarth (as a social satirist), Thomas Jefferson, Benjamin Franklin and Thomas Paine. To the Romantic poets themselves, however, and to many students of their movement, they were rebels against what they felt was an evil, the cold analytical reason of the preceding century—which they often symbolized by the serpent.

2. William Wordsworth, *Complete Poetical Works*. Student's Cambridge Edition (Boston, 1904), p. 83. (All quotations are from this edition.)

3. T. R. Henn, *The Apple and the Spectroscope* (London, 1951), p. 38.

4. Carveth Read, *Man and His Superstitions* (Cambridge, 1925), p. 69.

5. Maud Bodkin, *Archetypal Patterns in Poetry: Psychological Studies of Imagination* (London, 1951), p. 204, footnote 1.

6. Robert Penn Warren, *A Poem of Pure Imagination: An Experiment in Reading* (New York, 1946), p. 76.

7. C. S. Lewis, *The Allegory of Love* (Oxford, 1936), p. 45.

8. Ananda Coomaraswamy, "The Life of Symbols." *Modern Review*, LVII (February 1935), 226.

9. Ernest Jones, *Essays in Applied Psychoanalysis* (London, 1951), II, 126.

10. George Wingfield Digby, *Symbol and Image in William Blake* (Oxford, 1957), pp. 6-7.

11. Samuel Taylor Coleridge, *Anima Poetae* (London, 1895), p. 136.

12. Samuel Taylor Coleridge, *Biographia Literaria,* ed. Ernest Rhys (New York, 1934), ch. XIV, p. 167.

13. John Livingston Lowes, *The Road to Xanadu* (Boston, 1927), p. 48.

14. John Keats, *The Letters of John Keats,* ed. Maurice Buxton Forman ('London, 1952), Letter 25, p. 52.

15. John Keats, *Poetical Works*, ed. H. W. Garrod (London, 1956), p. 209. (All quotations are from this edition.)

16. Percy Bysshe Shelley, Preface to *The Cenci*, in *Complete Poetical Works*, ed. Thomas Hutchinson (London, 1952), p. 277. (All quotations are from this edition.)

17. V. F. Calverton, *Sex Expression in Literature* (New York, 1926), p. 158.

## Chapter Two

1. Blake, however, is the notable exception. Nature, according to this poet, provides no spiritual help for man but appeals only to his senses and reason. Thus, Blake distrusts and damns nature, which he compares to a deceiving serpent.

2. Keats, *The Letters of John Keats*, Letter 93, p. 227.

3. John Heath-Stubbs, *The Darkling Plain* (London, 1950), pp. xii-xiii.

4. Charles Lamb, "Witches, and Other Night Fears," *Essays of Elia* (London, 1884), p. 118.

5. Alexander Altmann, "Symbol and Myth," *Philosophy*, XX (July 1945), 163.

6. Thomas M. Raysor (ed.), *The English Romantic Poets* (New York, 1950), p. 240.

7. Lane Cooper, "The Power of the Eye in Coleridge," *Studies in Language and Literature in Honor of J. M. Hart* (New York, 1910), p. 98.

8. John Livingston Lowes, *The Road to Xanadu* (Boston, 1927), p. 254.

9. Charles Gould, *Mythical Monsters* (London, 1886), pp. 260-61.

10. Coleridge, *Biographia Literaria*, ch. XIV, p. 161.

11. Mario Praz, *The Romantic Agony* (London, 1933), p. 31.

12. *On the Medusa of Leonardo da Vinci*, v, p. 583.

13. Kenneth Burke, *The Philosophy of Literary Forms: Studies in Symbolic Action* (Baton Rouge, 1941), p. 63.

## Chapter Three

1. William Blake, *Complete Poetry and Prose*, ed. Geoffrey Keynes (London, 1956). *Vala, or the Four Zoas*, VIIb, p. 326. (All quotations are from this edition.) The other serpent images describing man's emotions: *Auguries of Innocence*, p. 119.

2. *The Prelude*, IX, *ll.* 569-78.

3. Samuel Taylor Coleridge, *Complete Poetical Works*, ed. Ernest Hartley Coleridge (Oxford, 1912). *The Destiny of Nations*, I, p. 136, Variant *ll.* 123-26. (All poetry quotations are from this edition.) The other serpent images describing man's emotions: *Love's Apparition*

*and Evanishment,* I, p. 489, *l.* 4. *The Nose,* I, p. 9, *l.* 31. *Zapolya,* II, Part II, III, i, *l.* 249.

4. Lord George Gordon Byron, *Complete Poetical Works.* Student's Cambridge Edition (Boston, 1933) *Don Juan,* II, ccxv. (All quotations are from this edition.) The other serpent images describing man's emotions: *Cain,* III, i, *ll.* 383-84. *Don Juan,* IV, lxi. *Manfred,* I, i, *ll.* 236-37. *The Giaour,* p. 322, *ll.* 1194-95. *Werner; Or, the Inheritance,* I, i, *ll.* 165-66; II, i, *ll.* 277-80; III, i, *ll.* 184-85.

For a more authoritative *Don Juan,* slightly different from the Student's Cambridge Edition, see the recent four-volume edition of W. W. Pratt and T. G. Steffan: *Byron's "Don Juan"* (Austin, Texas, 1957). In this edition, "Life knots" is "Like knots." See the explanation in Pratt's volume four.

5. *Alastor,* p. 20, *ll.* 226-37. The other serpent images describing man's emotions: *Music,* p. 657, *ll.* 9-10. *Oedipus Tyrannus,* p. 402, *ll.* 74-75. *Prince Athanase,* p. 161, *ll.* 121-23. *The Revolt of Islam,* II, iv, *ll.* 699-702; VIII, xxi, *ll.* 3385-87; X, xxxii, *ll.* 4076-78; XI, xxv, *ll.* 4442-43; XII, vii, *ll.* 4504-6.

6. *Hyperion,* I, *ll.* 259-63. The other serpent images describing man's emotions: *Endymion,* II, *ll.* 873-75; III, *ll.* 239-40; IV, *ll.* 66-71; IV, *ll.* 751-54. *Hyperion,* II, *ll.* 44-49. *Lamia,* I, *ll.* 131-33. *The Cap and Bells,* XXXVIII.

7. *Jerusalem,* I, 15, p. 449. The other serpent images describing man's physical and mental attributes: *Europe,* p. 212. *Jerusalem,* II, 40, p. 482. *Milton,* I, 13, p. 388. *The Book of Ahania,* III, p. 237. *The Book of Los,* IV, p. 245. *The Everlasting Gospel,* 2e, p. 141. *Tiriel,* 6, p. 159; 8, p. 161. *Vala, or The Four Zoas,* V, p. 295.

8. *Ecclesiastical Sonnets,* I, xxi, *ll.* 7-12. The other serpent images describing man's physical and mental attributes: *Ode: 1816,* p. 543, *ll.* 146-48. *Sonnets upon the Punishment of Death,* VI. *The Excursion,* III, *ll.* 850-52.

9. *Dejection: An Ode,* I, p. 367, *ll.* 94-95. The other serpent images describing man's physical and mental attributes: *Christabel,* I, p. 229, *ll.* 442-43; p. 233, *ll.* 583-87. *Parliamentary Oscillators,* I, p. 212, *ll.* 15-16. *Religious Musings,* I, p. 119, *l.* 286. *Remorse,* II, III, ii, *ll.* 81-82. *Sancti Dominici Pallium,* I, p. 448, *ll.* 7-9. *Sonnet,* I, p. 393, *ll.* 5-6. *To a Young Lady,* I, p. 66, *l.* 42.

10. *Last Words on Greece,* p. 206. The other serpent images describing man's physical and mental attributes: *Cain,* I, i, *ll.* 34-35; I, i, *ll.* 389-90. *Don Juan,* III, xlviii, *ll.* 379-80; IV, xlviii, *l.* 381; IV, xlvii, *ll.* 381-82. *Heaven and Earth,* I, i, *ll.* 126-28. *Mazeppa,* p. 412, *ll.* 533-36. *Sardanapalus,* II, i, *ll.* 165-66. *The Bride of Abydos,* p. 325, *ll.* 158-61. *The Deformed Transformed,* I, i, *ll.* 38-39; I, ii, *ll.* 805-6; I, ii, *ll.* 807-8; I, ii, *ll.* 857-58; III, i, *ll.* 107-8. *The Giaour,* p. 318, *ll.* 842-45; p. 319. *ll.* 896-98. *The Island,* p. 434, *ll.* 336-38.

11. *Queen Mab*, p. 771, *ll.* 61-62. The other serpent images describing man's physical and mental attributes: *Adonais*, p. 436, *l.* 196; p. 440, *ll.* 329-30. *Charles the First*, I, *ll.* 127-28. *Fragment: A Serpent Face*, p. 633. *Ode to Liberty*, p. 608, *ll.* 218-21. *Prometheus Unbound*, I, *l.* 632; III, iv. *ll.* 15-19. *The Cenci*, V, iii, *ll.* 136-37. *The Revolt of Islam*, IV, xix, *l.* 1584; V, xxv, *l.* 1941.

12. *Otho the Great*, V, ii, *ll.* 6-8. The other serpent images describing man's physical and mental attributes: *Endymion*, III, *ll.* 529-31. *Otho the Great*, III, ii, *ll.* 152-55; V, iv, *l.* 12. *The Fall of Hyperion*, I, *ll.* 446-47.

13. *Otho the Great*, III, ii, *ll.* 152-55.

14. *The Four Zoas*, VIII, p. 333.

Blake's opulent serpent is astonishingly similar to Milton's serpent as it moved toward Eve,

> his Head
> Crested aloft, and Carbuncle his Eyes;
> With burnisht Neck of verdant Gold, . . .
> (*Paradise Lost*, IX, *ll.* 449-501)

Blake's other serpent images describing the whole man: *America*, p. 201; p. 203; p. 204; p. 207. *Jerusalem*, I, 14, p. 448; II, 49, p. 495; III, 54, p. 501; III, 55, pp. 501-2. *Milton*, I, 5, p. 379; I, 13, p. 388. *The Book of Ahania*, IV, p. 239. *The First Book of Urizen*, VI, p. 229; IX, p. 233. *The Song of Los*, p. 248; p. 250. *Tiriel*, 1, p. 151; 4, p. 156; 4, p. 156; 6, p. 158; 8, p. 160. *Vala, or The Four Zoas*, I, p. 266; II, pp. 269-70; VI, pp. 303-4; VIIa, p. 313; VIIb, pp. 325-26; VIIb, p. 328; VIII, p. 341; VIII, p. 342; VIII, p. 344; IX, p. 348; IX, p. 349; IX, p. 349.

15. *The Prelude*, X, *ll.* 390-93. The other serpent images describing the whole man: *The Armenian Lady's Love*, XV. *The Borderers*, I, *l.* 527; III, *ll.* 121-22; III, *ll.* 288-91; III, *ll.* 445-49.

16. *Psyche*, I, p. 412. The other serpent images describing the whole man: *Christabel*, I, p. 233, *l.* 571. *Epigrams*, No. 25, II, p. 959; No. 26, II, p. 959. *Osorio*, II, III, *ll.* 213-15. *Religious Musings*, I, p. 119, *ll.* 274-76. *Remorse*, II, III, ii, *ll.* 96-98. *The Death of Wallenstein*, II, II, vi, *ll.* 54-56; II, III, vii, *ll.* 43-45. *The Destiny of Nations*, I, p. 144, *l.* 398; I, *l.* 146, *ll.* 435-39. *The Devil's Thoughts*, I, p. 320, *ll.* 9-12. *The Fall of Robespierre*, II, I, *ll.* 25-28; II, II, *ll.* 264-67. *Two Round Spaces on the Tombstone*, I, p. 355, *l.* 19. *Zapolya*, II, Part I, i, *ll.* 60-61; II, Part I, i, *ll.* 89-90; II, Part II, I, i, *l.* 176; II, Part II, I, i, *ll.* 258-59; II, Part II, I, i. *l.* 182; II, Part II, I, i, *l.* 234; II, Part II, i, *ll.* 11-12; II, Part II, IV, i, *ll.* 76-77.

17. *The Corsair*, I, xi, *ll.* 275-80. The other serpent images describing the whole man: *A Sketch*, p. 208, *ll.* 47-50. *Cain*, I, i, *ll.* 398-410; II, i, *ll.* 172-73; II, ii, *ll.* 300-7. *Heaven and Earth*, I, iii, *ll.* 856-59. *Marino Faliero*, III, ii, *ll.* 147-50; V, i, *ll.* 465-66. *The De-*

*formed Transformed,* I, i, *l.* 259; I, i, *ll.* 26-27. *The Irish Avatar,* p. 203, *ll.* 97-100. *The Prophecy of Dante,* I, *ll.* 63-68. *Verses Found in a Summer-House at Hales-Owen,* p. 171. *Werner; Or, the Inheritance,* I, i, *ll.* 83-88; II, ii, *ll.* 395-96; II, ii, *ll.* 447-59.

18. *Ode to Liberty,* p. 608, *ll.* 211-15. The other serpent images describing the whole man: *Adonais,* p. 437, *ll.* 236-40; p. 438, *ll.* 248-51. *Charles the First,* II, *l.* 212. *Julian and Maddalo,* p. 198, *ll.* 398-400. *Ode to Naples,* p. 618, *ll.* 83-84; p. 619, *ll.* 111-13. *Prometheus Unbound,* III, i, *ll.* 70-74. *Similes for Two Political Characters of 1819,* p. 573, *l.* 20. *The Cenci,* I, *ll.* 165-66; IV, iv, *ll.* 15-16; V, ii, *ll.* 27-28. *The Revolt of Islam,* I, xxix, *ll.* 383-84; I, xxxiii, *ll.* 420-23; II, xlvi, *l.* 1080; V, vii, *ll.* 1774-77; X, vii, *ll.* 3853-55. *To Edward Williams,* p. 644, *l.* 1.

19. *Endymion,* III, *ll.* 490-502. The other serpent images describing the whole man: *Isabella,* XXIV; *Lamia,* I, *ll.* 78-80. *Otho the Great,* IV, i, *ll.* 14-16.

20. *Europe,* p. 216. The other serpent images describing areas and aspects of man's life and experiences: *The French Revolution,* p. 167. *The Marriage of Heaven and Hell,* p. 181.

21. Blake uses "mortal errors" in the sense of "fatal errors."

22. *Ecclesiastical Sonnets,* III, xlvii, *ll.* 1-5.

23. *The Death of Wallenstein,* II, II, ix, *ll.* 51-56. The other serpent images describing areas and aspects of man's life and experiences: *Religious Musings,* I, pp. 115-16, *ll.* 173-78. *The Death of Wallenstein,* II, II, vi, *ll.* 76-78. *The Piccolomini,* II, IV, vii, *ll.* 250-53.

24. *Childe Harold's Pilgrimage,* I, lxv, *ll.* 661-65. The other serpent images describing areas and aspects of man's life and experiences: *Cain,* I, i, *ll.* 18-21; II, ii, *ll.* 494-504; III, i, *ll.* 401-4; III, i, *ll.* 427-30. *Childe Harold's Pilgrimage,* I, lv, *ll.* 573-74; IV, cxxxii, *ll.* 1183-85; IV, clx, *ll.* 1432-40. *Childish Recollections,* p. 127, *l.* 390. *Heaven and Earth,* I, iii, *ll.* 303-11. *Marino Faliero,* I, ii, *ll.* 449-52; III, ii, *ll.* 358-59. *Monody on the Death of The Right Hon. R. B. Sheridan,* p. 193, *l.* 86. *The Curse of Minerva,* p. 271, *ll.* 219-20.

25. *The Mask of Anarchy,* p. 342, *ll.* 226-29.

26. *The Revolt of Islam,* I, xxviii, *ll.* 370-76. The other serpent images describing areas and aspects of man's life and experiences: *Cancelled Stanza of An Ode,* p. 576, *ll.* 5-7. *Fragment: To The Mind of Man,* p. 635, *ll.* 15-17. *Ginevra,* p. 650, *ll.* 58-64. *Hellas,* p. 451, *ll.* 107-8; p. 451, *ll.* 145-46. *Marenghi,* p. 565, *ll.* 44-45. *Ode to Liberty,* p. 606, *ll.* 117-20. *Prometheus Unbound,* I, *ll.* 326-27; I, *ll.* 346-49; II, iii, *ll.* 91-97; III, i, *ll.* 39-42; IV, *ll.* 562-69. *Queen Mab,* p. 782, *ll.* 195-96; p. 791, *ll.* 238-39. *Rosalind and Helen,* p. 178, *ll.* 699-703. *The Cenci,* II, i, *ll.* 86-87; IV, *ll.* 179-80. *The Daemon of the World,* I, *ll.* 99-101. *The Revolt of Islam,* I, xxxiii, *ll.* 419-20; VIII, xxvii, *ll.* 3439-40; X, xxxviii, *ll.* 4133-34; XI, viii, *ll.* 4288-92.

27. *The Cap and Bells*, xxii.

28. *The Everlasting Gospel*, 2b, pp. 134-35. The other serpent images describing natural phenomena and man-made objects: *Europe*, p. 215; p. 217; p. 219. *Jerusalem*, II, 29, p. 469; II, 42, p. 486; IV, 80, p. 542. *Vala, or The Four Zoas*, III, p. 282; VI, p. 301; IX, p. 353.

29. Arthur Symons, *William Blake* (New York, 1907), p. 263.

30. *Ibid.*, p. 264.

31. *The Egyptian Maid*, p. 680, *ll.* 320-23. The other serpent images describing natural phenomena and man-made objects: *An Evening Walk*, p. 7, *l.* 246. *Desultory Stanzas*, p. 591, *l.* 63. *Dion*, p. 528, *ll.* 82-83. *The Excursion*, VII, *ll.* 47-48; VII, *ll.* 791-92. *The Prelude*, III, *l.* 563; VI, *ll.* 705-7. *The River Duddon*, IV. *Yew-Trees*, p. 292, *ll.* 16-18.

32. *Childe Harold's Pilgrimage*, IV, clxxiii, *ll.* 1155-57.

33. *Alastor*, p. 22, *ll.* 323-25. The other serpent images describing natural phenomena and man-made objects: *Adonais*, p. 435, *ll.* 161-62. *Alastor*, p. 24, *ll.* 438-41. *A Vision of the Sea*, p. 598, *ll.* 100-4. *Fragments of an Unfinished Drama*, p. 486, *ll.* 163-67. *Hellas*, p. 477, *ll.* 1060-63. *Mont Blanc*, p. 534, *ll.* 100-2. *Prometheus Unbound*, III, iii, *l.* 135; III, iv, *ll.* 119-21; IV, *l.* 291. *The Mask of Anarchy*, p. 340, *ll.* 110-11. *The Revolt of Islam*, I, lvi, *ll.* 622-24. *The Sensitive Plant*, III, *ll.* 51-53. *To Jane: The Recollection*, p. 669, *ll.* 21-24.

34. *Ode on Melancholy* (cancelled stanza), p. 398. The other serpent image describing natural phenomena and man-made objects: *Endymion*, IV, *ll.* 128-29.

35. *The First Book of Urizen*, I, p. 220. The other serpent images describing pictorial detail: *I Saw a Chapel All of Gold*, p. 87. *Jerusalem*, III, 73, p. 531; IV, 98, p. 567. *King Edward the Third*, p. 29. *Milton*, I, 29, p. 410. *The Book of Ahania*, IId, pp. 236-37. *The French Revolution*, p. 168; p. 180. *The Ghost of Abel*, p. 584. *To Nobodaddy*, p. 93. *Visions of the Daughters of Albion*, p. 196; p. 200.

36. *Fort Fuentes*, p. 582, *ll.* 7-8. The other serpent images describing pictorial detail: *The Excursion*, II, *ll.* 41-47. *When Philoctetes in the Lemnian Isle*, p. 651.

37. *The Picture*, I, p. 369, *ll.* 4-6. The other serpent images describing pictorial detail: *Christabel*, I, p. 232, *ll.* 549-54. *Duras Navis*, I, p. 3, *l.* 38. *Melancholy*, I, p. 74, *l.* 6. *The Night Scene*, I, p. 423, *ll.* 82-83.

38. *Cain*, I, i, *ll.* 220-24.

39. Genesis 3: 1 (King James version. All quotations are from this version.)

40. *Cain*, I, i, *ll.* 226-29. The other serpent images describing pictorial detail: *Cain*, I, i, *ll.* 191-92; I, *l.* 459; II, iii, *ll.* 395-400. *Darkness*, p. 189, *ll.* 35-37.

41. *Prometheus Unbound*, IV, *ll.* 305-8. The other serpent images describing pictorial detail: *A Vision of the Sea*, p. 599, *ll.* 137-44. *Cancelled Fragments of Prometheus Unbound*, p. 268. *Marenghi*, p. 567, *ll.* 89-90; p. 567, *ll.* 106-7. *Prometheus Unbound*, II, v, *l.* 43; III, iv, *ll.* 36-39; III, iv, *ll.* 73-75. *Rosalind and Helen*, p. 169, *ll.* 113-19; p. 169, *l.* 132. *The Cenci*, III, i, *ll.* 46-47. *The Daemon of the World*, II, *ll.* 377-79; II, *ll.* 379-83. *The Revolt of Islam*, I, xix, *ll.* 289-94; V, I, *ll.* 2162-63; X, iii, *ll.* 3815-18; X, xliii, *l.* 4176; X, xlv, *ll.* 4193-94. *The Witch of Atlas*, p. 373, *ll.* 89-93. *Wake the Serpent Not*, p. 586, *ll.* 1-4.

42. *Lamia*, I, *ll.* 45-65. The other serpent images describing pictorial detail: *Fancy*, p. 214, *ll.* 57-58. *Fragment*, p. 397, *ll.* 15-16.

## Chapter Four

1. Blake, *Complete Poetry and Prose*, p. 818.

2. *Ibid.*, p. 821.

3. Claude Lee Finney, *The Evolution of Keats's Poetry* (Cambridge, Mass., 1936), II, 699.

4. *Lamia*, II, *ll.* 304-11.

5. In this chapter, see the remarks on Pantheism for another discussion of the image of the water snakes.

6. *The Rime of the Ancient Mariner*, I, IV, *ll.* 272-87.

7. John Livingston Lowes, *The Road to Xanadu* (Boston, 1927), p. 48.

8. Newton P. Stallknecht, "The Moral of the 'Ancient Mariner,'" *PMLA*, XLVII (June 1932), 561.

9. Robert Penn Warren, *A Poem of Pure Imagination: An Experiment in Reading* (New York, 1946), p. 103.

10. Sir James George Frazer, *The Golden Bough* (London, 1917), VIII, 146-47.

11. Matthew 10:16.

12. *The Revolt of Islam*, IV, xix, *ll.* 1583-84.

13. *The Egyptian Maid*, p. 680, *ll.* 320-23.

14. Miriam J. Benkovitz, "The Good Serpent," *Folk-Lore Society of London, Transactions*, LXI (September 1950), 149.

15. *The Revolt of Islam*, I, xxviii, *ll.* 373-76. This image has been discussed in chapter III under Areas and Aspects of Man's Life and Experiences.

16. M. Oldfield Howey, *The Encircled Serpent* (New York, 1955), pp. 75-76.

17. *Lamia,* I, *ll.* 131-33.
18. *Endymion,* IV, *ll.* 66-71.
19. Ovid, *Metamorphoses,* trans. Frank Justus Miller (London, 1928), II, ix, 21-23.
20. *Endymion,* III, *ll.* 237-40.
21. *Hellas,* p. 477, *ll.* 1060-63.
22. Howey, *op. cit.,* p. 226.
23. Marjorie Hope Nicolson, *The Breaking of the Circle* (Evanston, Ill., 1950), p. 34.
24. *The Daemon of the World,* p. 3, *ll.* 99-101.
25. *Fragment: To the Mind of Man,* p. 635, *ll.* 15-17.
26. *Ecclesiastical Sonnets,* III, xlvii, *ll.* 1-2.
27. *Prometheus Unbound,* II, v, *l.* 43.
28. *The Excursion,* II, *ll.* 41-47.
29. *When Philoctetes in the Lemnian Isle,* p. 651.
30. *The Rime of the Ancient Mariner,* I, IV, *ll.* 272-87.
31. Stallknecht, *loc. cit.*
32. Warren, *loc. cit.*
33. E. M. W. Tillyard, *Five Poems, 1470-1870* (London, 1948), p. 76.
34. D. H. Lawrence, "Reptiles," in *Birds, Beasts and Flowers* (New York, 1923), pp. 106-7.
35. *The Daemon of the World,* II, *ll.* 379-83.
36. *Marenghi,* p. 567, *ll.* 106-7.
37. *The Witch of Atlas,* p. 373, *ll.* 89-93.
38. *Jerusalem,* IV, 98, p. 567.
39. *The Ghost of Abel,* p. 584.
40. *Cain,* I, i, *ll.* 191-92.
41. *Cain,* I, i, *ll.* 220-25.
42. *Cain,* I, i, *ll.* 227-29. The images are discussed in Chapter III, under Pictorial Detail.
43. *Cain,* I, i, *ll.* 397-402.
44. Nolan B. Harmon (ed.), *The Interpreter's Bible* (New York, 1952), I, 501.
45. *To Nobodaddy,* p. 93.
46. *Cain,* I, *ll.* 34-35.
47. *Jerusalem,* III, 55, pp. 501-2. For an analysis of these and many other symbols, see: *The Prophetic Writings of William Blake,* ed. D. J. Sloss and J. P. R. Wallis (Oxford, 1926).
48. *Vala, or The Four Zoas,* VIII, p. 341.
49. David G. Downey (ed.), *Abingdon Bible Commentary* (New York, 1929), p. 222.
50. *The Bride of Abydos,* p. 325, *ll.* 158-61.
51. *Heaven and Earth,* I, iii, *ll.* 856-59.
52. *To Edward Williams,* p. 644, *l.* 1.

53. Newman Ivey White, *Portrait of Shelley* (New York, 1945), p. 442.

54. *To Jane: The Recollection*, p. 669, *ll.* 21-24.

55. Edith Hamilton, *Mythology* (New York, 1942), p. 70.

56. *Endymion*, III, *ll.* 490-502. The imagery is discussed in chapter III, under The Whole Man.

57. *Christabel* is evidence that Coleridge was acquainted with lamia lore. However, the poem is not discussed here, because it deals with a woman beguiling a woman rather than a man. This poem is discussed in this chapter under the heading Man Against Man.

58. Robert Burton, *The Anatomy of Melancholy* (London, 1883), p. 494.

59. *Lamia*, I, *ll.* 45-65. The image is discussed in chapter III, under Pictorial Detail.

60. *Jerusalem*, I, 15, p. 449.

61. *Jerusalem*, III, 54, p. 501.

62. *The French Revolution*, p. 167.

63. *Dejection: An Ode*, I, p. 367. An analysis of this image appears in chapter III under the category dealing with man's physical and mental attributes.

64. *Europe*, p. 216.

65. *Jerusalem*, II, 49, p. 495.

66. *Milton*, I, 5, pp. 379-80.

67. *Vala, or The Four Zoas*, III, p. 282.

68. *Jerusalem*, II, 29, p. 469.

69. Symons, *op. cit.*, pp. 297-98.

70. Thomas Bulfinch, *Mythology* (New York, 1913), p. 15.

71. *Prometheus Unbound*, IV, *ll.* 305-8. The image was discussed in chapter III, under Pictorial Detail.

72. *The Book of Los*, IV, p. 245.

73. *Jerusalem*, I, 15, p. 449. The image was discussed in chapter III under Man's Physical and Mental Attributes.

74. *Vala, or The Four Zoas*, VIII, p. 333. The image is discussed in chapter III, under The Whole Man.

75. *Jerusalem*, II, 49, *ll.* 67-71.

76. *Werner, or The Inheritance*, II, i, *ll.* 277-80.

77. Frazer, *op. cit.*, IV, 132-33.

78. *Otho the Great*, III, ii, *ll.* 152-55. The image is discussed in chapter III under Man's Physical and Mental Attributes.

79. *The Cenci*, V, iii, *ll.* 136-37.

80. *The Death of Wallenstein*, II, II, vi, *ll.* 54-56.

81. *Sardanapalus*, II, i, *ll.* 165-66.

82. *Sonnet* I, p. 393, *ll.* 5-6. Coleridge's translation of a sonnet by Giambattista Marini (Marino).

83. *Christabel*, I, p. 232, *ll.* 549-54.

84. *Christabel*, I, p. 233, *ll.* 579-87.
85. *The Deformed Transformed*, I, i, *ll.* 26-27.
86. *The Deformed Transformed*, I, i, *l.* 39.
87. *Tiriel*, I, p. 151.
88. *The Ghost of Abel*, p. 584.
89. *The Revolt of Islam*, V, vii, *ll.* 1774-77.
90. *Ginevra*, p. 650, *ll.* 58-64.
91. *Prometheus Unbound*, IV, *ll.* 562-69.
92. *Adonais*, p. 437, *ll.* 236-40.
93. *Adonais*, p. 438, *ll.* 248-51.
94. *Adonais*, p. 438, *ll.* 253-61.
95. *Adonais*, p. 440, *ll.* 329-30.
96. *The Witch of Atlas*, p. 371, *ll.* 1-4.
97. *The Revolt of Islam*, X, vii, *ll.* 3853-55.
98. Frazer, *op. cit.*, IV, 86-87.
99. *The French Revolution*, p. 180.
100. *The Prophecy of Dante*, I, *ll.* 63-68.
101. *The Fall of Robespierre*, II, II, *ll.* 264-67. Coleridge and Southey are joint authors of this drama.
102. *The Irish Avatar*, p. 203, *ll.* 97-100.
103. *Marino Faliero, Doge of Venice*, I, ii, *ll.* 449-52.
104. *Marino Faliero, Doge of Venice*, III, ii, *ll.* 358-59.
105. *Marino Faliero, Doge of Venice*, III, ii, *ll.* 148-50.
106. *Dion*, p. 528, *ll.* 82-83.
107. *Ode to Liberty*, p. 608, *ll.* 217-23. For discussion of a similar image—also from *Ode to Liberty*—see chapter III under The Whole Man.
108. Matthew 23: 33.
109. *I Saw a Chapel All of Gold*, p. 87.
110. *The Revolt of Islam*, X, xxxii, *ll.* 4076-78.
111. *Rosalind and Helen*, p. 178, *ll.* 699-703.
112. *Vala, or The Four Zoas*, VII, b, pp. 325-26.
113. Preface, *The Revolt of Islam*, p. 32.
114. *The Revolt of Islam*, X, xlv, *ll.* 4189-97.
115. *Milton*, I, 13, p. 388.
116. *Milton*, I, 13, p. 388.
117. *Jerusalem*, IV, 80, p. 542.
118. *Europe*, p. 215.
119. Blake, *Complete Poetry and Prose*, p. 927.

## Chapter Five

1. Other breakdowns of serpent imagery are, of course, possible. There could be, for example, a classification according to subject matter, such as history, mythology, politics, and religion; another

could be a classification according to the senses stimulated, such as the visual, auditory, olfactory, gustatory, tactile, and kinesthetic.

2. George Wingfield Digby, *Symbol and Image in William Blake* (Oxford, 1957), p. 23.

3. Coleridge, *Biographia Literaria*, ch. XIV, p. 165.

4. Douglas Bush, *Mythology and the Romantic Tradition in English Poetry* (Cambridge, Mass., 1937), pp. 43-44.

# Bibliography

# Bibliography

## Primary Sources

BLAKE, WILLIAM. *Complete Poetry and Prose,* ed. GEOFFREY KEYNES. London: The Nonesuch Library, 1956.

————. *The Prophetic Writings,* ed. D. J. SLOSS and J. P. R. WALLIS. 2 vols. Oxford: Clarendon Press, 1926.

BYRON, LORD GEORGE GORDON. *Complete Poetical Works.* Student's Cambridge Edition. Boston: Houghton Mifflin, 1933.

————. *Byron's "Don Juan,"* ed. W. W. PRATT and T. G. STEFFAN. (Variorum edition of "Don Juan" with historical commentary and volume of notes.) 4 vols. Austin: University of Texas Press, 1957.

COLERIDGE, SAMUEL TAYLOR. *Anima Poetae.* London: William Heinemann, 1895.

————. *Biographia Literaria,* ed. ERNEST RHYS. New York: Dutton, 1934.

————. *Complete Poetical Works,* ed. ERNEST HARTLEY COLERIDGE. 2 vols. Oxford: Clarendon Press, 1912.

KEATS, JOHN. *The Letters of John Keats,* ed. MAURICE BUXTON FORMAN. 4th ed., revised. London: Oxford University Press, 1952.

————. *Poetical Works,* ed. H. W. GARROD. London: Oxford University Press, 1956.

SHELLEY, PERCY BYSSHE. *Complete Poetical Works,* ed. THOMAS HUTCHINSON. London: Oxford University Press, 1952.

WORDSWORTH, WILLIAM. *Complete Poetical Works.* Student's Cambridge Edition. Boston: Houghton Mifflin, 1904.

## Secondary Sources

ALTMANN, ALEXANDER. "Symbol and Myth," *Philosophy,* XX (July 1945), 162-71.

BENKOVITZ, MIRIAM J. "The Good Serpent," *Folk-Lore Society of London, Transactions,* LXI (September 1950), 146-51.

BODKIN, MAUD. *Archetypal Patterns in Poetry: Psychological Studies of Imagination.* London: Oxford University Press, 1951.

BULFINCH, THOMAS. *Mythology.* New York: Crowell, 1913.

BURKE, KENNETH. *The Philosophy of Literary Form: Studies in*

*Symbolic Action*. Baton Rouge: Louisiana State University Press, 1941.

BURTON, ROBERT. *The Anatomy of Melancholy*. London: Chatto and Windus, 1883.

BUSH, DOUGLAS. *Mythology and the Romantic Tradition in English Poetry*. Cambridge, Mass.: Harvard University Press, 1937.

CALVERTON, V. F. *Sex Expression in Literature*. New York: Boni & Liveright, 1926.

COOMARASWAMY, ANANDA. "The Life of Symbols," *Modern Review*, LVII (February 1935), 224-26.

COOPER, LANE. "The Power of the Eye in Coleridge," in *Studies in Language and Literature in Honor of J. M. Hart*. New York: Holt, 1910.

DOWNEY, DAVID G. (ed.). *Abingdon Bible Commentary*. New York: Abingdon-Cokesbury Press, 1929.

FINNEY, CLAUDE LEE. *The Evolution of Keats's Poetry*. 2 vols. Cambridge, Mass.: Harvard University Press, 1936.

FRAZER, SIR JAMES GEORGE. *The Golden Bough*. 12 vols. London: Macmillan, 1917.

GOULD, CHARLES. *Mythical Monsters*. London: W. H. Allen & Co., 1886.

HAMILTON, EDITH. *Mythology*. New York: New American Library, 1942.

HARMON, NOLAN B. (ed.). *The Interpreter's Bible*. 12 vols. New York: Abingdon-Cokesbury Press, 1952.

HEATH-STUBBS, JOHN. *The Darkling Plain*. London: Eyre & Spottiswoode, 1950.

HENN, T. R. *The Apple and the Spectroscope*. London: Methuen, 1951.

Holy Bible. King James Version. Edited by the American Revision Committee. Standard Edition. New York: T. Nelson & Sons, 1901.

HOWEY, M. OLDFIELD. *The Encircled Serpent*. New York: Arthur Richmond Co., 1955.

JONES, ERNEST. *Essays in Applied Psychoanalysis*. 2 vols. London: Hogarth, 1951.

LAMB, CHARLES. *Essays of Elia*. The Temple Edition. London: Putnam's, 1884.    .

LAWRENCE. D. H. "Reptiles," in *Birds, Beasts and Flowers*. New York: Thomas Seltzer, 1923.

LEWIS, C. S. *The Allegory of Love*. Oxford: Clarendon Press, 1936.

LOWES, JOHN LIVINGSTON. *The Road to Xanadu*. Boston: Houghton Mifflin, 1927.

MILTON, JOHN. *Paradise Lost,* ed. MERRITT Y. HUGHES. New York: Odyssey Press, 1935.

NICOLSON, MARJORIE HOPE. *The Breaking of the Circle*. Evanston, Ill.: Northwestern University Press, 1950.

OVID. *Metamorphoses*. 2 vols. Translated by FRANK JUSTUS MILLER. London: Putnam's, 1928.

PLINY. *Natural History*. 10 vols. Translated by H. RACKHAM. Cambridge, Mass.: Harvard University Press, 1940.

PRAZ, MARIO. *The Romantic Agony*. London: Oxford University Press, 1933.

RAYSOR, THOMAS M. (ed.). *The English Romantic Poets*. New York: Modern Language Association of America, 1950.

READ, CARVETH. *Man and His Superstitions*. Cambridge: Cambridge University Press, 1925.

STALLKNECHT, NEWTON P. "The Moral of the 'Ancient Mariner,'" *PMLA*, XLVII (June 1932), 559-69.

SYMONS, ARTHUR. *William Blake*. New York: Dutton, 1907.

TILLYARD, E. M. W. *Five Poems, 1470-1870*. London: Chatto & Windus, 1948.

WARREN, ROBERT PENN. *A Poem of Pure Imagination: An Experiment in Reading*. New York: Reynal & Hitchcock, 1946.

WHITE, NEWMAN IVEY. *Portrait of Shelley*. New York: Knopf, 1945.

WINGFIELD DIGBY, GEORGE. *Symbol and Image in William Blake*. Oxford: Clarendon Press, 1957.